P9-EJO-481

Wood Bender's
HANDBOOK

Zachary Taylor

Sterling Publishing Co., Inc.
New York

Library of Congress Cataloging-in-Publication Data Available

10 9 8 7 6 5 4 3 2 1

Published by Sterling Publishing Company, Inc.
387 Park Avenue South, New York, N.Y. 10016
© 2001 by Zachary Taylor
Distributed in Canada by Sterling Publishing
℅ Canadian Manda Group, One Atlantic Avenue, Suite 105
Toronto, Ontario, Canada M6K 3E7
Distributed in Great Britain and Europe by Cassell PLC
Wellington House, 125 Strand, London WC2R 0BB, England
Distributed in Australia by Capricorn Link (Australia) Pty Ltd.
P.O. Box 6651, Baulkham Hills, Business Centre, NSW 2153, Australia
Printed in China
All rights reserved

Sterling ISBN 0-8069-9702-8

684. 08

THOUSAND OAKS LIBRARY

3 2052 00754 9127 ✓

JAN   2002

DISCARD

Wood Bender's
H A N D B O O K

Collection Management

7/03	3	6/03
10/06	5 1	02/05
10/09	10 — 1	11/08
6/20/18	12 – 1	7/201

THOUSAND OAKS LIBRARY
1401 E. Janss Road
Thousand Oaks, CA 91362

This book is dedicated to my old friend Jack Hill,
a Great British craftsman

ACKNOWLEDGMENTS

Thanks are due, primarily, to you Dear Reader, for taking up this book. To those who progress beyond this page, it will become clear that several people contributed, directly or indirectly, to my efforts. Grateful thanks to you all, including:

Barry Barrett-Mold of Aylesbury College, for research and woodworking facilities

Geoff and **Martin Brown** of BriMarc, for bending equipment and other woodworking tools

Kirk Boulton of Craft Supplies, for timber

Sean Fallon of Tramex, for the supply of Moisture Meters

John Faulkner of the Phoenix Walking Stick Company, for the invitation to photograph his stick-making process

Bob Forsyth, for his rib-bending demonstration

Jack Hill, for my visit to photograph his chair-making course

Dan Holman of the Adjustable Clamp Company, for a range of clamps

Jane Julier, for inviting me into her workshop to photograph her bending methods

Leonard Leigh of Veritas, for wood-bending equipment and other woodworking tools

James Marston, for photographs of his work

Nick Smyth of Chairworks, for my visit to photograph gardening baskets and chairs

Roy Tam of Trannon, for photographs of their bent-wood products

CONTENTS

Wood-Bending Projects and Demonstrations 97

INTRODUCTION

When it comes to bending wood— whether for components for musical instruments, furniture, boats, or much more—those without experience may be understandably cautious, perhaps even over-awed when approaching the subject. Many questions will arise, and they will probably include: What is the best wood for the job? Should it be wet? Should it be steamed? Should it be boiled? Should it be "green"? What techniques and equipment are involved?

An essential question is: Does the wood need to be bent? After all, it is possible to achieve a curve in a piece of wood just by cutting away the waste to leave a bent shape, isn't it? This is so, but there are very good reasons why certain bent shapes should not be made this way, as will become clear from the information in this book.

That some woods bend more easily than others will be obvious when comparing an ebony walking stick with a greenheart fishing rod, or a hickory ax shaft with a long-bow made of yew. Of course, the length and section of the material also play a part in its flexibility, as may be seen in the examples given in this book, but nevertheless, some woods are more obliging than others when persuading them to accept a bend. Bending the selected member to the required shape is still only part of the process; making it retain that shape is another matter and equally important. All is revealed in the following pages.

This particular book is intended to inform about the theories and techniques of wood bending, with detailed instructions to achieve a wide variety of applications. It is not a project book as such, but, hopefully, it will enable the creation of many kinds of bent-wood items, including parts for musical instruments, furniture, and domestic articles. In short, once the principles are understood, a vast range of applications should be at the reader's disposal.

Fortunately, no great expense need be incurred in setting up a bending operation; the greater need is the ability to grasp some

Some musical instruments made by the author. At the back, an organistrum with ribs bent in English walnut. From left to right, a lute in bird's-eye maple; a medieval fiddle in olive wood; a Torres model guitar in Brazilian rosewood; a mandolin in figured maple, a Panormo guitar in sycamore, and a Borch hurdy-gurdy in lacewood. Lacewood is the name given to London plane (English) or sycamore (American).

A selection of garden baskets produced via wood bending.

Walking sticks are a popular wood-bending project.

simple techniques and the willingness to accept some failures during the learning process. From time to time, disappointment may attend even the most experienced craftsman.

Unlike many woodworking techniques, successful wood bending relies more on correct preparation than on the actual bending operation. In other words, if all the considerations of material selection, sizing, and correct application of the equipment have been observed, then there is a fair chance of success, provided that the essential ingredient "good fortune" is also included. As always, we try to eliminate the need for the latter, wherever possible. So, for those with a need to create a beautiful shape, a functional member, or an item that combines both, by bending wood, please read on.

The author, Zachary Taylor, framed in a set of rosewood guitar ribs bent by John Davies, one of his students.

PART ONE

Wood-Bending Principles and Techniques

Chapter 1

BASIC INFORMATION

WHY BEND WOOD?

In the days when ships and boats were made primarily of wood, the shipwright, faced with the task of fitting curved members, would try to choose timber that was "grown" to the required shape (1–1). Frames and "knees" made from trees and branches that had natural curves needing little work to shape them correctly were, therefore, highly prized.

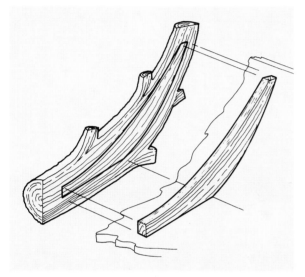

1–1.   A "grown" knee, showing how a bent boat member might be cut from a tree trunk.

If the shape or size of the required pieces could not be matched with "grown" limbs, there were two other possibilities: either cut the shapes from solid pieces or bend them. Curved shapes cut from a wide board are not a realistic option because they not only waste raw material but they may well be weak due to the presence of short grain occurring somewhere in the curvature (1–2).

Considering bending as an alternative, wood has a limited flexibility in its "dry" state and, therefore, before it is bent it must be prepared, either by kerfing, laminating, boiling, steaming, or treating with chemicals such as anhydrous

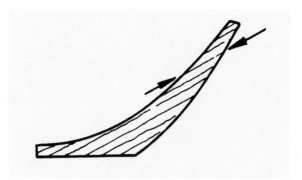

1–2.   If a bent shape similar to that shown in 1–1 were to be cut from a plank, like as not there would be a "short" grain section, as shown, at which point breakage would occur.

ammonia. The last method is beyond the scope of this book and will therefore be disregarded.

All of the aforementioned methods are capable of increasing the natural flexibility of wood, and they each have their virtues and shortcomings. An examination of each method will help newcomers to the subject decide on the choice most appropriate for their needs. Examples are given for the practical uses of each method in chapters 3 and 4.

BENDING CHARACTERISTICS OF WOOD

Wood is mankind's oldest natural and renewable resource. As well as providing us with fuel, shelter, and tools, wood has enhanced our lives in countless ways with its beauty when used in works of art and craft (1–3 to 1–5). Wood varies enormously in its physical characteristics, not only from one species to another but also from one tree to another of the same family. Variations may be found between two parts taken from the same tree, and even within one small piece. This lack of consistency may be regarded as an asset or a disadvantage, depending on one's point of view.

1–3. An armchair made from young hazel sticks, bent while "green" and fixed with nails. Traditional techniques applied to a traditional material.

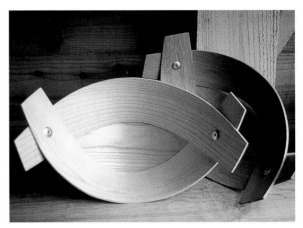

1–5. James Marston's crafts are handmade with refinement based on natural rustic harmony.

1–4. Steam-bent from locally grown ash, this functional and elegant stacking chair by Trannon is an excellent example of the combination of contemporary elements in a traditional item, with a design appropriate to the choice of material.

As with all green plants, trees make the materials used for growth by a process called photosynthesis (1–6). Not that there is much talk of this process among woodworkers, but it is essential to have some knowledge of the structure of wood from, literally, the ground up.

Photosynthesis, in simple terms, is a process in which water is taken from the earth and combined with carbon dioxide taken into the leaf from the air to produce its food. Water, carrying nutrients from the soil, enters the tree system through its roots and then travels up through the tubes in the sapwood to the crown of the tree.

Wood is, therefore, already multipurpose in its functions: as a conductor of water, a food processor, a reproductive organ, and a structural material supporting the living tree.

By far the most prominent components used to make the material for wood growth are cellulose and lignin. Cellulose and lignin are intimately related, but the early wood found in the seasonal growth ring contains more lignin than cellulose. Lignin may constitute as much as 30 percent in softwoods and about 20 percent in hardwoods. It is possible that this characteristic contributes to the greater difficulty in success-

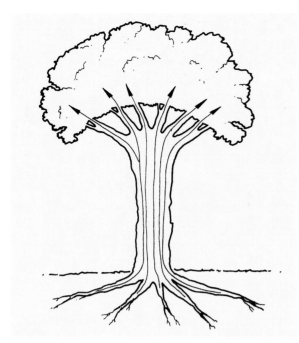

1–6. A diagram of a tree, showing the movement of nutrient-bearing water drawn from the soil and conveyed through the tree system.

ful bending of softwoods. Wood is produced in layers called cambium that envelope the tree under its bark (1–7).

The inner part of cambium grows and attaches to the already dying heartwood, and the

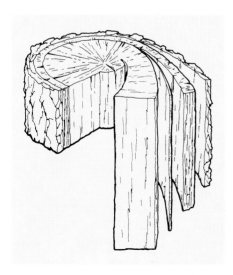

1–7. An exploded view of a section of a tree trunk. From the outside: the bark, cambium, sapwood, and heartwood.

outer part grows and attaches to the new layer immediately beneath the bark. Seasonal growth such as is found in trees grown in temperate zones is seen as growth rings, usually one per year. Tropical regions have continuous growth and, therefore, trees growing there seldom show growth rings. If the tree grows steadily upwards, rather than deviating erratically, it is likely to produce a straight trunk with a correspondingly straight grain; this is a desirable characteristic for bending.

Woods that are naturally "springy," such as yew or some varieties of cane, are used to advantage in cases where resilience is needed, such as for an archery bow or a fishing rod (1–8). Here are good examples of bends attainable, demonstrating that the major task facing the wood-bending operator is to prevent the wood's returning to its original form.

Resilience varies, as do other characteristics, from one wood species to another; in some ways, it depends on the wood's particular physical structure. Resilience in wood is connected with the amount of air it contains, along with other factors. Wood has a natural ability to overcome deformation and return to its original shape once the stress has been removed. In the bending process, it is necessary to overcome this resilience in order to deform the material. So, having coaxed the workpiece to accept a bend by whatever method, it then becomes necessary to fix it in its curved position permanently. This will be explained as part of the bending techniques described in later chapters.

Although wood itself is not very "elastic," the compression of air in its cells assists in its recovery after being deformed. Wood of low density, that is, lightweight wood, has thin-walled cells and low resilience, resulting in failure under stress with permanent deformation. This wood is fine for bending as long as it is not crushed in the operation. It may be assumed

that the higher the density of the wood, the greater its elasticity. For example, greenheart at 12 percent moisture content—considered "dry" in general terms—is approximately twice as hard as beech, but it is also twice as "elastic."

Those with access to supplies of freshly felled green wood have several advantages, including the possibility of producing "riven" workpieces. Riven stock is split from green billets and is ideal for the production of items of random sizes or those requiring less precision in thickness and width. Garden furniture designed to take advantage of the rustic appearance of natural timber comes to mind. Some shaping can be carried out by sawing after bending and drying, but the advantage of the riven piece is that it follows the grain line, unlike a piece that is sawn. When a piece is riven, or split, from a billet, a tool called a "froe" is used; this tool, when correctly applied, is cap-

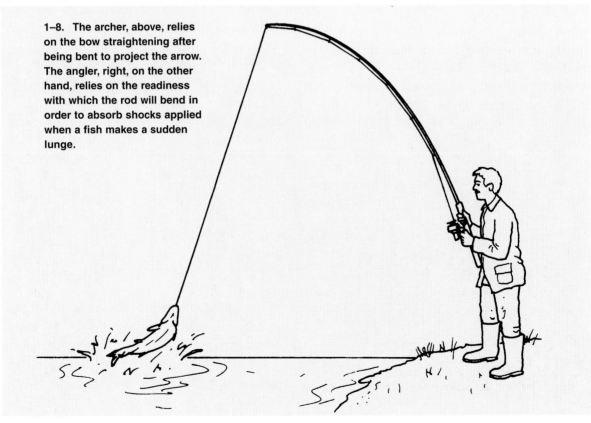

1–8. The archer, above, relies on the bow straightening after being bent to project the arrow. The angler, right, on the other hand, relies on the readiness with which the rod will bend in order to absorb shocks applied when a fish makes a sudden lunge.

able of producing a relatively straight slat or plank of uniform thickness (1–9 and 1–10).

Such pieces can be bent immediately while the sap content is high and the bend can be set, provided that it can be restrained for several days, even for weeks, until completely dry. Holding a bent member until it is set is a question of providing a mold or form for the purpose. Alternatively, several bent pieces may be attached to each other, each contributing restraint to adjacent pieces. These methods are explained in chapter 6.

The success of the riving method depends entirely on the quality of the section of the tree from which the billet was taken. Flawless, knotless, straight, even-grained, and fresh-felled specimens are unlikely to come the way of most woodworkers, so this method of preparation will not be used in this book.

Ideally, the wood for any bending operation will be straight-grained, without flaws, and of dimensions suitable for the job. What represents a flaw in the wood is in respect to its suitability for bending rather than its color or aesthetic qualities. Some defects may be acquired by natural process, some from ill treatment, and some from mishandling during felling or seasoning. Any suspected defect should be inspected in detail. Pieces with any of the following features are best rejected, or set aside for some other purpose:

1. Knots (1–11). Knots are left by a branch that has been cut from, or broken off, a tree trunk. The grain in the main part will have diverted around this obstacle, creating problems of workability and weakness. If a limb breaks off when immature, the knot may become hidden

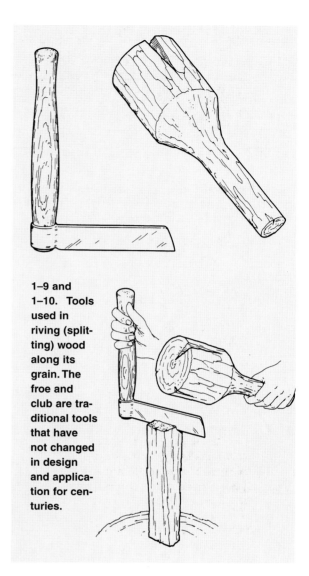

1–9 and 1–10. Tools used in riving (splitting) wood along its grain. The froe and club are traditional tools that have not changed in design and application for centuries.

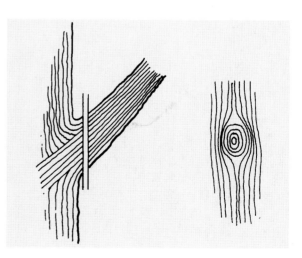

1–11. When a branch is severed from the trunk, a knot is formed, causing the grain to divert as it grows around the defect.

when cambium grows over it in a healing process. Unfortunately, this fault may escape notice until it is too late to avoid problems in the bending operation. Knots of one-half inch or less in diameter are accepted in timber intended for general purposes and graded as "prime." Such a defect would not be allowable as a piece for bending unless it were for use as a relatively large member, say for a boat plank, but better to set it aside in preference for a knotless specimen. Even if it were possible to bend the plank successfully, the danger remains of the knot shrinking and falling out.

2. Shakes (1–12). "Shakes"—sometimes called "splits"—occur either during the tree's growth or, more usually, during seasoning. Stresses held in tension while a tree is growing are often released when it is felled. Clearly, a tree growing on a hillside develops a tendency to lean over. It follows that the upper side of the trunk will be in tension and its lower side is in compression. When felled, such a specimen will almost certainly develop a multitude of faults during seasoning as the stresses are relieved. This applies to all branch wood that grows horizontally from a main trunk and is, therefore, best avoided if stability is essential. If a tree succeeds in overcoming gravity and grows upright, as Alpine spruces do, for instance, then it will grow with equilibrium in its trunk.

Whole planks may develop shakes at their ends after being sawn to size, and this is due to their drying out too quickly. Retarding the process of drying can help prevent this happening, and dipping the plank ends into wax or painting them will help achieve this (1–13 to 1-15).

1–13. Ends of larger workpieces are easily painted with melted paraffin wax and a brush for economy.

1–14. A simple setup for coating the ends of workpieces. The saucepan contains melted paraffin wax, previously heated in another, larger vessel filled with hot water. The double saucepan is to reduce the risk of fire. A disposable foam applicator is used to paint the ends with the hot wax.

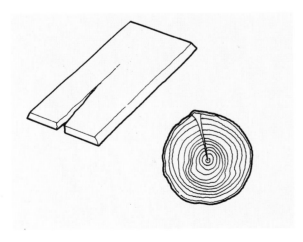

1–12 (left). Various events and conditions cause shakes or splits, but the effect is the same—to ruin the possibility of structural use where the fault occurs.

1–15. Smaller workpieces may be dipped in a tin of melted wax for speed and efficiency if a quantity has to be protected.

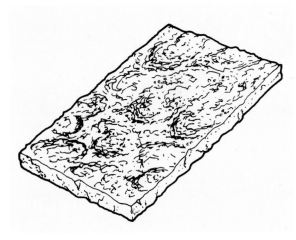

1–16. A burr, shown here as useful for decorative features, is also an example of material that presents major problems as a bending element.

3. *Burrs* (1–16). Burrs are often not classified as defects, but usually represent prized features and may enhance the value of the timber, but not for bending! Often as not the burr, or burl, arises from a pollarded (or severely trimmed) crown of the tree, or by failure of small twigs to develop. Sometimes attack by fungus or insects can produce a type of burr, but this usually occurs at the base of the trunk.

4. *Cupping, bowing, spring, and twist* (1–17). These are all terms that describe some of the faults arising from warping. Warping can occur not only during the seasoning of the wood, but also at later stages. Because wood shrinks as it dries and swells as it gains moisture, it is fair to assume that wood is never completely stable. It will always be undergoing slight dimensional changes due to fluctuations of humidity and temperature of the surrounding air.

Any changes in the shape and size of a given workpiece due to shrinkage are not uniform. Shrinkage is greatest along the growth rings, only about one half as much across the growth rings, and minimal along the length of the grain. This is known as tangential, radial, and longitudinal shrinkage, respectively. In general, the greater the density of the timber, the greater the shrinkage.

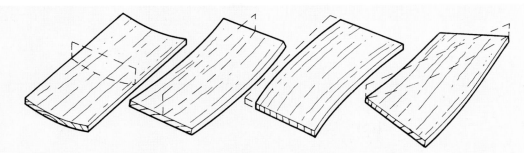

1–17. All of these examples are characteristic of common defects found frequently in wood cut into boards. From left to right: cupping, bowing, spring, and twist.

MOISTURE CONTENT

Accurate measurement of moisture in timber should be regarded as important to every woodworker and not only the wood bender. Take the case of the cabinetmaker who creates a cupboard or chest using boards of different moisture content. Within a short time after completion when the components have reached a uniform level of moisture content, some will probably have warped because of imbalance during construction. Imbalance results from greater expansion, or contraction, of one component attached to another causing movement of the composite structure. One possible and easy solution would be to store the material as basic stock in the workshop for a sufficient time to achieve uniform moisture content before work on it is started.

Moisture content is expressed as a percentage of the dry weight of timber. Dry weight of a given material means the lowest weight achievable, and this is readily available by oven-drying methods. The specimen must be weighed prior to drying, then enclosed in an oven, subjected to heat, and weighed regularly until its lowest weight is achieved. Assuming the original weight of the specimen was 12 pounds and its oven-dry weight 10 pounds, then the water loss is 2 pounds in 10; therefore, its moisture content was 20 percent. A formula might be expressed thus: Original weight – dry weight × 100 = Moisture Content.

"GREEN" WOOD

When considering "green" wood—which has not been fully seasoned by air- or kiln-drying methods—a definition is called for. Green wood is generally considered to be in a state where its cell walls are completely saturated. Note: the cell walls are saturated, but no water is present within the cell cavity. This condition is also known as the "fiber saturation point," assumed for practical purposes to be about 30 percent. Of course individual specimens may differ. One specimen, a piece of hornbeam $2 \times 2 \times 36$ inches, varied in moisture content by 4 percent from one end to the other. This was measured by applying a moisture meter.

MOISTURE METERS

Verifying the moisture content by the oven method described above is somewhat cumbersome and time-consuming, but with a moisture meter the problem may be solved accurately and quickly.

Modern moisture meters are handheld, battery-powered instruments, with a digital readout showing moisture content (1–18). One type measures the electrical resistance between a

1–18. A variety of moisture meters, including one with a software disc and computer connection. The latter enables 625 readings to be transferred to a computer for analysis in spreadsheet form or incorporated into word processing.

pair of electrodes pressed into the surface of the wood (1–19). Several sizes of moisture meter are available, including one small enough to carry on a wrist strap with a protective cap covering the electrode pins when not in use. One model that will appeal to most craftsmen is a noninvasive one that uses coplanar electrodes that transmit low-frequency signals into wood to a depth of about three quarters of an inch (1–20). This allows the moisture meter to be slid over the surface of the material, registering the moisture content and any variations over the whole piece. The readout is by digital display with a built-in temperature sensor.

As for wood that comes to the user already "dry" or "seasoned," it is important to ascertain, if possible, whether it has been air- or kiln-dried. Currently, kiln drying is favored, for eco-

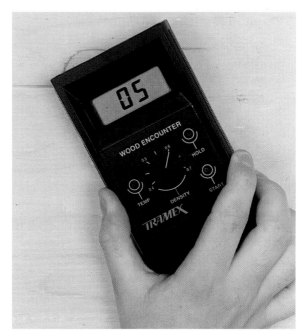

1–20. A noninvasive moisture meter that is simply placed on the wood surface to give moisture content on a digital readout. Adjustment for different specific gravity is available to suit various woods, and a temperature sensor is incorporated for better accuracy.

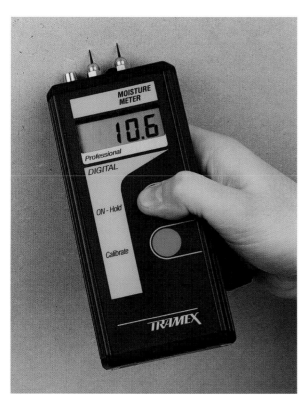

1–19. A digital probe-type of resistance meter available with separate deep-probe electrodes detachable for remote contact.

nomic, commercial, and practical purposes. Kiln drying is satisfactory for most common purposes, but wood bending is not a common woodworking operation and kiln-dried timber is not considered to be ideal for this job. It would not be too difficult to find someone experienced in wood bending who has successfully used kiln-dried materials. It is done frequently, not so surprisingly because, as was stated earlier, most timbers are supplied in a kiln-dried condition with no alternative available. However, this does not alter the firmly held opinion that drying by exposure to air is believed to produce a superior material for bending.

Some experts consider that kiln drying can induce minute surface cracks by case-hardening the timber, and that this may lead to rupturing under stress. Add to this the well-supported theory that drying in a kiln hardens the lignin, rendering steaming or boiling less effective.

Wood that has been dried, by whatever means, to less than 10-percent moisture content will be difficult to bend successfully because the lignin is permanently set and cannot be plasticized completely by a steaming treatment.

Air-drying may be regarded as a "natural" process if the timber is simply stacked under some shelter that provides protection from precipitation with open sides to admit the free flow of air (1–21). In this case, the moisture content would be higher than kiln-dried wood, though this would not be detrimental for the bending operation. In most cases, the wood to be bent is likely to be immersed in water, sometimes boiled in water, or subjected to steaming, so its moisture content when acquired is, within normal limits, relatively unimportant.

Special preparations such as these will be dealt with in subsequent chapters, as required by the particular bending methods.

1–21. These bundles of chestnut are waiting to dry indoors with ample air circulating to continue their seasoning, having been stacked outside in a shelter for some months.

SAFETY CONSIDERATIONS

As with any other workshop activity that uses tools, specialized equipment, and heat in various forms, there is some risk of personal injury if caution is not observed.

It has been detailed in many parts of the book that heat is necessary to change the shape of wood by bending it in its natural form. Whether the required heat is applied to the workpiece by means of direct contact or by means of immersion in water or steam, some basic care should be taken.

In direct contact, as in the case of the use of a bending iron for shaping ribs for a musical instrument, the iron, if it is hot enough to soften the material for bending, will obviously also burn the hands of the user if they are brought into contact with, or even close to, the hot surface. Use of a "strap" as shown in 1–22 helps to hold the wood firmly against the iron with greatly reduced risk of burnt hands.

If for any reason no strap or other device is applicable, then gloves should be worn as a protection against the heat and also to protect the hands in case of a workpiece breaking when under the duress of bending. Due to the unpredictable nature of wood, even if care is taken when choosing sound examples, there is always the possibility of an accident. See the demonstration in 1–23. If a workpiece breaks under stress for whatever reason, it is usually an unexpected occurrence and, therefore, the operator may be caught off-balance and fall. Moral: don't be caught off-guard, expect a possible accident, and be prepared to respond safely.

Steam is potentially dangerous in all its forms, whether generating it, ducting it, or storing it for the steaming operation itself. Steam is sneaky, being invisible; it scalds on contact and by the time its effect on flesh is felt, it is too late to avoid injury, the damage

1–22. Working close to the end of the rib portion of a musical instrument is difficult to manage without risk of burned fingers. The metal strap shown here protects the fingers and helps to prevent undesirable breakout of fibers on the outside of the bend.

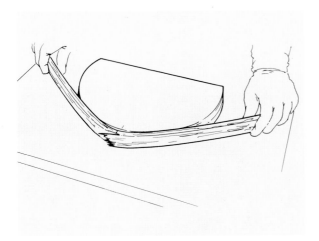

1–23. There is always the possibility of wood breaking when it is being bent, so care must be taken.

having been done. Therefore, when generating steam by heating water, there are several dangers to menace the unwary.

Taking the management of the heat source initially, this may be by flame applied to a water container or by an immersion heater. Flame produced by gas, oil, wood, or any other fuel-burning method is in a category all its own when it comes to potential disaster. Every pos-sible precaution should be taken to ensure that the fire source complies with safety regulations applicable to that specific appliance.

Containing the water while heating it to produce steam and maintaining its tempera-ture for the required duration to provide suffi-cient steam for the bending operation needs special attention. Presuming that some kind of container is used as a boiler, the volume of the boiling water is reduced as steam is generated, or, in simple terms, it boils away. So, it follows that the container should be large enough to hold sufficient water for the operation or it should have some means of adding more water if necessary. Bear in mind that if the water has boiled away, leaving the container dry and hot, the addition of cold water would almost cer-tainly result in an explosion (refer to chapter 10). As an extra safeguard, when replenishing water in the boiler, it is prudent to add it at near its boiling point. This not only assists in the continuous generation of steam but it also considerably reduces the risk of instantly con-verting the boiler into a ballistic missile.

Ducting the steam is the next item in the chain of steam application. Every care should be taken to ensure that the ducting material, such as pipe or flexible hose, is clear and free of obstruction. It is best if it is inclined upwards from the water vessel to the steam chamber to allow condensation moisture to run back. Any leaking joints in the system should be regarded as not only inefficient but also potentially dan-gerous. Containing the steam in the steam chamber presents a lesser hazard, provided that there is at least one hole with a partial seal to prevent pressure buildup.

If the boiler is installed with an immersion heater, similar to a tea urn or pot, or to a do-mestic hot-water tank, there is another perilous potential. The two essential components used in the process of steam generation by this means, water and electricity, become companions if they are allowed to mix. Every joint in the boiler should be scrupulously examined for leaks, especially the one around the immersion heater mounting. All electrical terminals and the power cable should be in good order with correct fuses connected to suit the equipment. Every precaution should be taken to shield the system from moisture and condensation. It is sensible to wear gloves made from insulating fabric as a protection from electric shock and hot water during the whole procedure.

A further wise safety precaution is to conduct a "dry run" before commencing on the bending project properly. This simply means setting up the equipment and materials and going through the motions of the project without heat, to verify the procedure, observing, among other aspects, the considerations of safety.

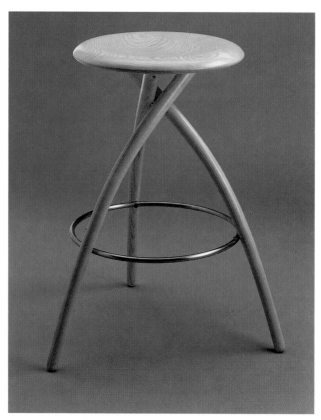

This chair—a superb example of a wood-bent design—was probably made with the clamp-and-mold technique described in chapter 6.

Chapter 2

DESIGN PRINCIPLES AND CONSIDERATIONS

When designing for bent wood, it would be helpful to refer to the preceding chapter to help understand the nature of the material and its behavior during the bending operation.

There are many questions to answer, all of which will be dealt with in detail as each technique appears in the book. For the moment, let us approach the matter by considering specific items that can be wood bent and design approaches when making them. A list of items might include walking sticks, skis, boat planks, furniture components, and parts for musical instruments (2–1 and 2–2). The list need not end there, but let it suffice for the present purpose. All of the aforementioned items have dif-ferent uses and, therefore, the materials used need to be evaluated accordingly. Thus, the natural characteristics of a piece of sweet chestnut chosen for a walking stick would be inappropriate for the sides of a violin. This does not mean that such an instrument would fail to perform satisfactorily, but, as far as this writer knows, no respected violin exists with sweet chestnut sides. Pieces chosen for boat planking might not have the beauty demanded by furni-ture makers for their chairs, although oak and ash might well be used for both. Ash also is used, as well as hickory, for sporting items such as hockey sticks since these woods accept hard knocks better than most.

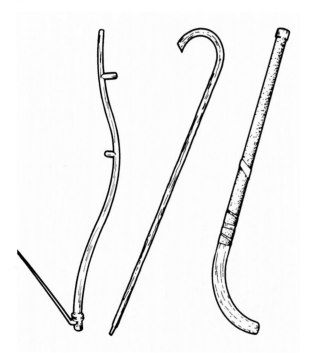

2–1. **Examples of artifacts of bent wood: a scythe handle, a walking stick, and a hockey stick.**

2–2. **A blend of traditional techniques with current trends, this elegant rocking chair is the work of Jack Hill, more of which is detailed in chapter 11.**

Table 2–1 contains a list of items that can be wood bent and the most common woods used for them.

Table 2–1

Items	Ash	Cherry	Chestnut	Hickory	Maple	Oak	Rosewood	Yew
Archery bows	🌳							🌳
Boat planks	🌳					🌳		
Boat ribs	🌳					🌳		
Chair parts	🌳	🌳	🌳	🌳	🌳	🌳		🌳
Garden baskets (trugs)	🌳		🌳					
Musical instruments sides		🌳			🌳		🌳	
Skis, for water or snow	🌳		🌳					
Tool handles	🌳		🌳	🌳				
Walking sticks	🌳	🌳	🌳	🌳				

Sometimes a bent member is used to connect two or more other parts, as in the case of ribs binding together the planks of a boat. In this example, the planks themselves are bent to make the shape of the boat (and also to keep out the water!). In both cases, there is the major need for structural strength combined with some resilience to cope with the stresses imposed by the movement of the vessel (2–3). Part of the design formula in this situation will attempt to reduce these stresses to as little as possible by shaping the contour of the hull's shape so as to reduce the resistance of the water to the forward motion of the boat. Streamlining, in a word. That is a subject beyond the scope of this book, but fortunately, technical information is available in the writing of authors who specialize in the topic, together with plans detailing shapes and sizes of all the components needed.

In this book all the examples given are of workpieces bent along the grain rather than across it. Perhaps it is unnecessary to state that wood may be bent across the grain but normally only for lightweight pieces such as applied decorative veneers.

VISUAL APPEARANCE

The visual appearance of wood-bent items varies in importance, depending on the purpose of the item. For example, a plain walking stick used as a aid to assist a patient with a temporary disability such as a broken leg needs merely to be rigid and strong to give confidence to the user. There is no need for it to be flawless—without cracks, shakes, or knots. A person with a permanent disability, however, whose stick might be a constant companion, would probably prefer it to have some attractive grain pattern or distinctive color (2–4).

Most musical instruments will be judged by their tone production primarily, but their ap-

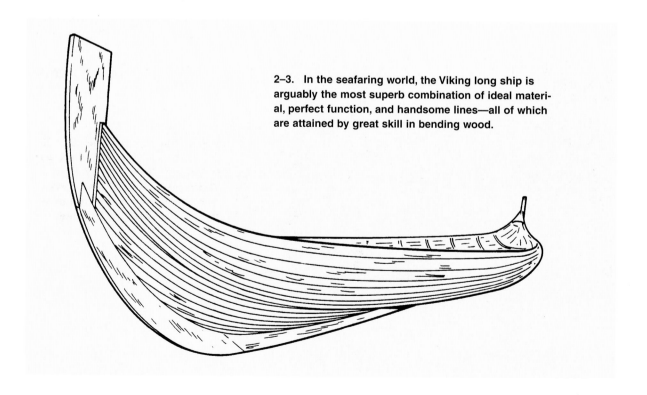

2–3. In the seafaring world, the Viking long ship is arguably the most superb combination of ideal material, perfect function, and handsome lines—all of which are attained by great skill in bending wood.

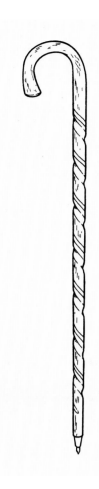

2–4. Decorated walking sticks are fashionable in many parts of Europe, especially in areas where hiking or climbing is found.

pearance is also something to be admired. Take a look at the back and sides of a fine guitar or a lute and see how the material has been selected for its spectacular appearance, or alternatively, for its subtlety (2–5 to 2–11). Here, the valuable benefit of diversity in the appearance of the material plays its part.

In many cases where the bent item is a visible component, it may be desirable to select material for its color and grain structure. Whether it should contrast with, or match, the adjacent components is a matter for individual judgment, or the dictates of fashion, if such a thing applies to this topic. Almost always, the back and sides of a guitar or violin will match, sometimes even being cut from the same log to ensure they look the same.

Bent pieces used in furniture are frequently made of a different material from that of the other parts, as in the bent back and the seat of a dining chair. Often the seat will be of elm and the back of beech. These two woods may be chosen because of a similarity in color, or at least of the same tone range, sufficient to be coordinated for this purpose. Differences in

(Text continues on page 34)

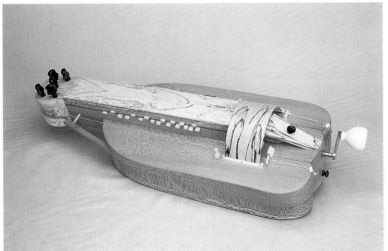

2–5. A reconstruction of the hurdy-gurdy that is depicted in the "Garden of Earthly Delights," a painting by Hieronymous Bosch. The materials include lacewood for the bent sides and spalted beech for the wheel cover.

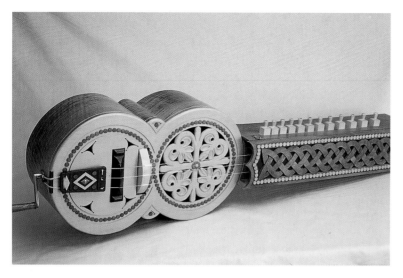

2–6. This is the famous "Organstrum," reproduced from examination of the twelfth-century sculpture at the entrance of the cathedral of Santiago de Compostela in Spain. The bent sides and main parts are from European walnut. The light- colored woods are spruce with decorations in ebony.

2–7. An original lute by Hans Frei, a sixteenth-century German luthier, was the inspiration for this reproduction. The back of the lute, consisting of 11 segments, is bird's-eye maple. The neck is made of walnut veneer, and the tuning pegs of holly. The lute is detailed in the author's book *Make and Play a Lute*.

2–8. Luis Panormo was of Italian extraction living in London in the eighteenth century and who made Spanish-style guitars. This multicultural influence was responsible for very fine instruments, one of which was used as a model to recreate the example shown here. The sides are bent from maple, with a spruce soundboard. The decorative trim is ebony. It is one of several instruments appearing in the author's book *Making Early Stringed Instruments*.

2–9. Copied from early designs researched in Europe, the body of this "figure-eight" fiddle was made in olive wood. The back is made from 12 pieces of olive, "book-matched" to emphasize the grain characteristics.

2–10. Interest in the flat-backed mandolin has revived, particularly in the area of folk and rustic music. This model, designed by the author, is intended for student makers. Its bent ribs are made from English sycamore, with rosewood trim.

2–11. Probably the most popular instrument of all time, the classic guitar. This Spanish-style instrument, designed and made by the author, features a Brazilian rosewood back and sides with decorative inlays.

the appearance of the grain would not matter too much in such an application, but it does not follow that the chosen materials could be used in reverse roles. The handsome piece of seasoned elm with the occasional knot and the swirling grain, if reduced to slender square sections, would almost certainly give trouble if used in a bending application. But that is a factor concerned with function and suitability.

EQUIPMENT AND DESIGN

"Know thy equipment" is a phrase that might be taken from the bible of woodworking techniques, if there is such a thing. While familiarity with wood-bending equipment is not considered a factor in design, nevertheless it is crucial to the viability of producing the required item. Even the best steam-producing plant combined with high-quality bending equipment will not help if it were under capacity for the project. As is so often the case, when setting out to plan a practical project, the primary factors include the limitations of the tools, workspace, time available, and knowledge of the subject. These must be considered alongside the dimensions and type and features of the material. In whichever sequence the design elements are resolved, when they are combined to produce the desired item, there will almost certainly be the need for compromise or adjustments: compromise in the choice of material due to available size or type; adjustments to the tools or methods available.

CALCULATING BENDING DIMENSIONS

What are the dimensions of a bend in expressible terms: radius, angle, and developed length? There are several ways to determine this infor-

mation: by measuring a full-size drawing, by calculation, or by creating a wire model from an existing member. A pattern traced from an original may be produced on a trial-and-error basis without the need for applied geometry. Alternatively, an uncomplicated geometrical construction may be used to verify the radius, angle, and length of the bend, if a drawing is available from which to verify these elements by inspection. Illus. 2–12 shows a simple eight-stage way to provide this relevant information. Using these steps, the angle, radius, and length of the bend can be determined as follows:

A. The angle of the bend aie may be measured with a protractor. Assume for the sake of the hypothesis that the angle is 36 degrees.

B. The radius may be measured with a ruler. Assume this to be 40 inches.

C. The length of the arc ae can be calculated with the following information: The angle aie is assumed to be 36 degrees, the equivalent of one-tenth of the circumference of the circle. The radius (40 inches) multiplied by 3.142 (the approximate equivalent of the Greek symbol

2–12 (next page).   Steps used to verify the radius, angle, and length of a bend. 1: An arc that is part of a circle is drawn. Its radius and length are unknown. 2: A line is drawn to connect the two ends of the arc (a and b). This line is called a chord. 3: A pair of compasses are used to draw arcs on each side, and from each end, of the chord. This produces crossed arcs whose centers, c and d, are arranged symmetrically and equidistant from the chord. 4: Connecting c and d bisects the line ab. 5: a and e are connected to produce chord ae.

6: One of the properties of a circle is that any angle connecting the ends of the centerline to its circumference makes a right angle. So, by reversing that rule, a line is drawn from a to f at a right angle. It follows that where the line af intersects with the line dc, point f must be a point on the circumference of a circle. Further, the line ef must represent the diameter of the circle. 7: From points f and e, arcs are scribed with a pair of compasses giving points of intersection g and h. These are joined to bisect the line ef. 8: A circle may now be drawn with its center at i and point e on its circumference; lines ia and ie are radii.

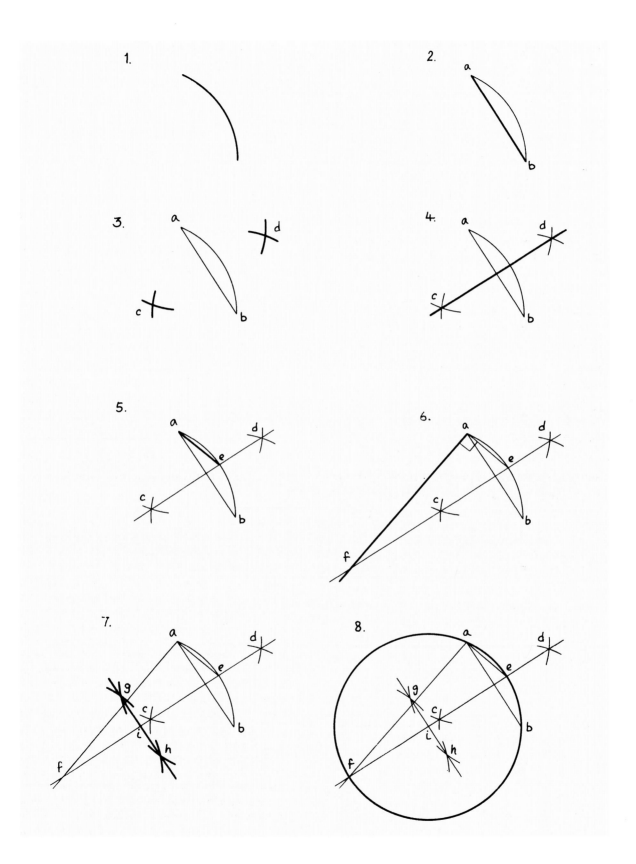

"pi") gives a circumference of 125.68 inches. One-tenth of this is 12. 568 inches, the length of the arc.

Most bends are "arcs," that is, a continuous portion of a curved line, such as part of the circumference of a circle. It is necessary to know what the radius is and the thickness of the chosen material in order to determine whether or not it will support the intended radius.

Bends are not always part of a circle; they may be elliptical, or part of an ellipse. Maybe the bend is convex or concave, or perhaps it combines both? What if there are two bends in compound angular planes? Illus. 2–13 shows how to deal with these considerations.

A piece of bent wood in its finished state may well be much shorter than the original workpiece from which it was made. In some cases, this is due to the need to grip an end, sometimes both, to work the bending process. These ends would usually be discarded after bending the item (2–14).

However, one of the physical facts of bending wood and its changing dimensions is this: since the convex side of the bend is formed with very little extension, the concave side is therefore, of necessity, compressed. This compression results in effectively shortening the workpiece on the inside of the bend. For example, a workpiece 1 inch square and 12

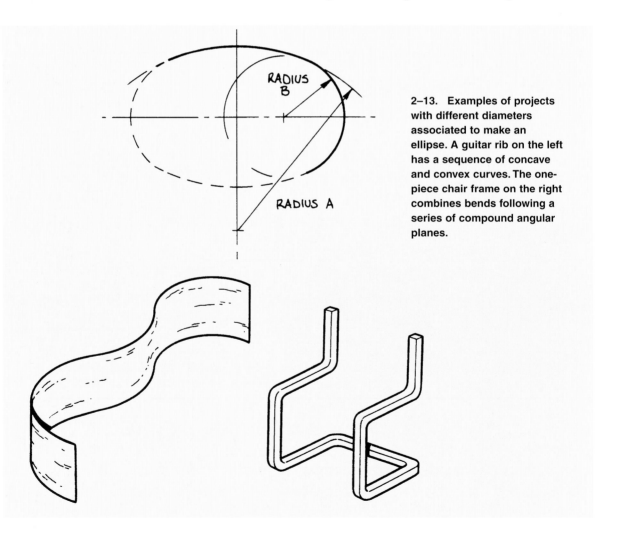

2–13. Examples of projects with different diameters associated to make an ellipse. A guitar rib on the left has a sequence of concave and convex curves. The one-piece chair frame on the right combines bends following a series of compound angular planes.

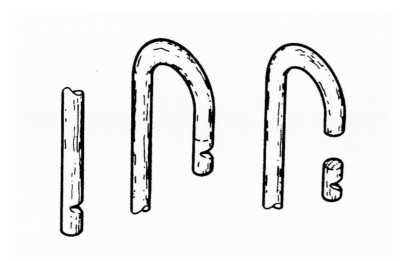

2–14. Spare material used to assist in the bending operation is trimmed off when the bending is completed.

inches long, if bent 90 degrees on a 6-inch radius, "loses" 1¾ inches on the inside curve (2–15)!

Using the theoretical data described in the section "The Effect of Bending on Wood" in chapter 3, it is possible to calculate the required thickness from a known radius or calculate the achievable radius from a known thickness.

As to its width and thickness, if the section of the member were rectangular rather than square, or oval rather than round, then this de-

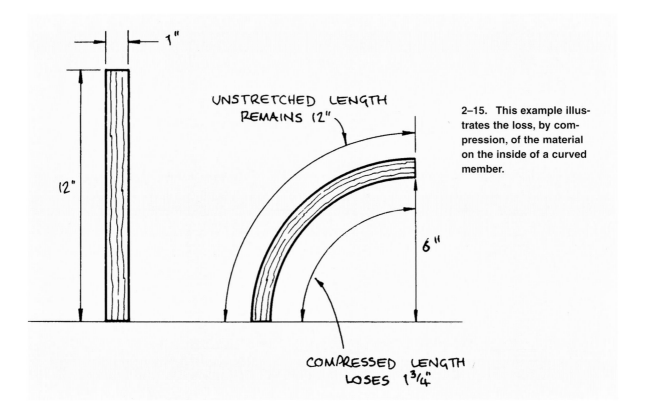

UNSTRETCHED LENGTH
REMAINS 12"

1"

12"

6"

COMPRESSED LENGTH
LOSES 1¾"

2–15. This example illustrates the loss, by compression, of the material on the inside of a curved member.

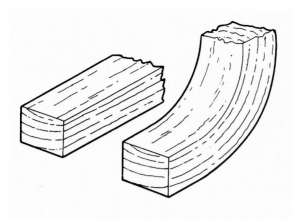

2–16. Here the bend follows the grain flow.

growth ring, delamination might occur. It is worth noting that there are excellent examples of this principle being ignored with spectacular success, in some cases due to blessed ignorance and sometimes because there is no alternative.

Some bends are slight, as in the case of some boat planking, but the size of the material adds its own problems (2–17). Imagine the size of chamber required to steam several planks for an old-time sailing boat and the amount of steam required to keep it filled for over an hour! Other methods are used to bend these planks.

Other bends are acute, such as in the small radii found in parts of a violin side, but the relatively thin section allows these parts to be easily bent with applied heat (2–18).

termines the axis that the bend should follow. In fact, the grain "flow" and its "orientation" may determine the direction of the bend (2–16). If bending a workpiece across the

2–17. A slender skiff might be made of relatively thin planks that might be bent without steaming.

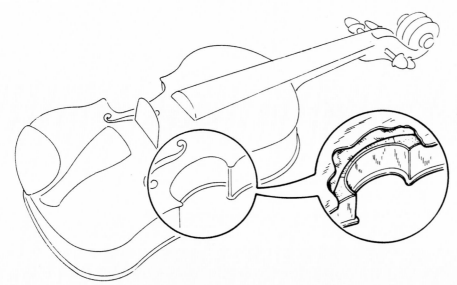

2–18. Some parts that make up the sides of a violin, particularly the in-curved ones at the waist, are only about $1/16$ inch and easily induced to bend with some applied heat. See chapter 5 for additional information.

Recliner chair and footstool by Trannon. This was the inaugural design that established the Trannon workshop in 1976. It is now part of a collection of twentieth-century furniture exhibited by Victoria and Albert Museum of London.

Chapter 3

BENDING METHODS

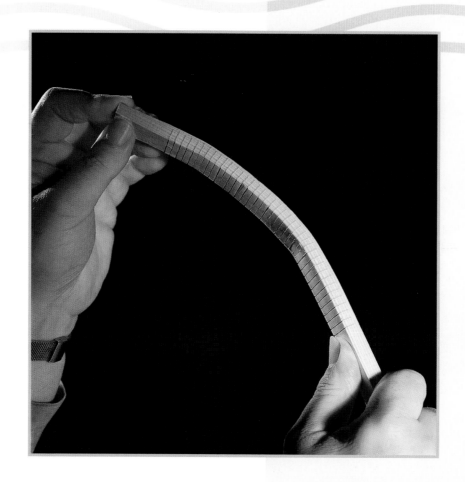

Consideration of the advantages and disadvantages of the various bending methods should be undertaken when designing the parts to be bent, the curvature of the bend, the size of the item, and the use to which it will be put.

To help with deciding on the most suitable bending method, it is wise to study the basics of each. The sections on pages 42 to 55 and chapters 4 to 6 describe these methods, which include dry bending, lamination, kerfing, hot bending with water or steam, hot-pipe bending, and bending with a clamp and mold.

THE EFFECT OF BENDING ON WOOD

Bending wood, in whatever state, whether hot, cold, wet, or dry, is a process that causes the deformation of the natural structure of the material by stretching and compressing it simultaneously. To clarify the apparent ambiguity of this statement: a curve, however slight, imposed on a naturally straight member causes compression of the material on the concave face, that is, the "inside" of the radius, while, theoretically, the fibers are stretched on the convex face, its "outside" (3–1). This situation assumes a neutral axis in the center of the member. A "neutral," or "static," axis is neither stretched nor compressed.

This theory applies to any flexible material and is a physical law. Unfortunately, wood stretches very little, relatively speaking, and this factor limits the extent to which it can be bent. In other words, the fibers tear on the outside of the curve when they have been subjected to a greater tension than they can bear. Almost all of the deformation is, therefore, undertaken by the compression of the material on the inside of the curve. To achieve this, a "strap-and-stop" method is applied. Stops are wooden blocks fixed to each

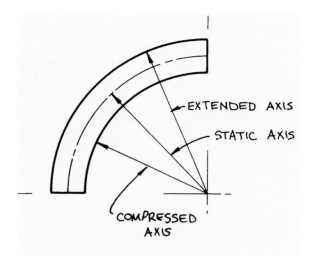

3–1. Three axes are shown in the example: the outer, extending axis, the inner, compressing axis, and between them, the neutral or static axis. It is emphasized that this is a theoretical situation that does not apply to an unsupported bent wood workpiece as is fully explained in the accompanying text.

end of a metal strap just wide enough apart to accept the length of the workpiece. When the bending commences, the strap presses against the outer surface of the bend, helping to prevent the fibers splintering; at the same time, the blocks reinforce this action by preventing the workpiece extending (3–2). This achieves the force to compress the cells on the inside curve as the material is bent around a mold.

If the outer line of the radius is restricted to prevent extension of the material, then all of the effort will be converted to compress the cells on the inner radius. By this technique, the neutral axis is transferred from the theoretical centerline to the concave, or outer, radius.

Without the application of the strap-and-stop system, or something similar, cells being compressed on the inside of the curve may collapse and crumple, creating a series of ridges, rather than the smooth surface that is normally required. This can happen, sometimes due to

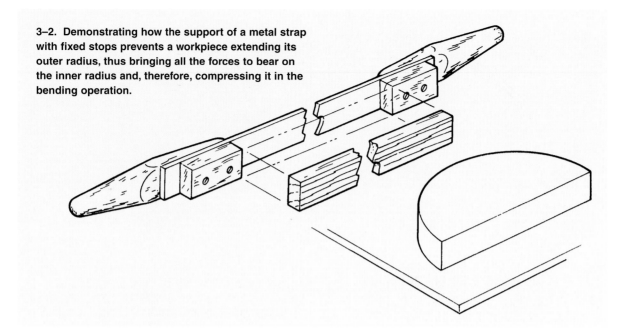

3–2. Demonstrating how the support of a metal strap with fixed stops prevents a workpiece extending its outer radius, thus bringing all the forces to bear on the inner radius and, therefore, compressing it in the bending operation.

oversteaming, even if the correct equipment is used. Such a fault may be correctable if the deformation is not excessive, by smoothing out the wrinkles with an abrasive.

HOT AND COLD BENDING

Even with the strap-and-stop system described above, there are limits to the degree of curvature and the radius achievable before rupture of the workpiece occurs. There are also other factors that should be taken into account. These include the type of material and its thickness and whether hot- or cold-bending methods will be used on the material. Hot bending is a method is which the wood is heated before bending. It is described in this chapter and chapters 4 and 5. Cold bending consists of any of several methods of bending wood that do not use heat. These methods include laminating the wood, cutting kerfs in it, and bending it without any treatment whatsoever. The latter is referred to as dry bending. These cold-bending methods are described in this chapter.

But even if wood bending is not a precise science, a rough and ready formula for calculating the radius of the material being bent may be created by using known factors and some that are based on experience and common sense. This formula is detailed in "Dry Bending" on pages 44 and 45. What is important to understand is that for a given specimen of 1 inch thickness, for example, cold bending could produce a 50-inch radius before rupturing occurs. A similar specimen if bent while hot might achieve a smaller radius of 12½ inches.

Even allowing for various contingencies, some acting for and some against the success of the operation, the potential difference between hot and cold bending is clear. Add to this the fact that it is necessary to use a metal strap or other device to prevent the bent workpiece from extending farther after it has reached the required curvature. In the case of hot bending, this device can be added after the wood has cooled. As has been mentioned elsewhere, this device would be needed during the entire cold-bending operation, because the wood would return almost to its original shape when

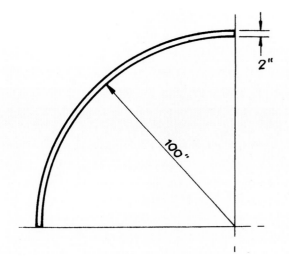

3–3. In the above illustration, the vast differences between heated and cold bending can be readily seen in the recommended radii available for a given section of similar material.

the bending force is released. Illus. 3–3 demonstrates the difference in radius when cold and hot bending a similar material.

Tables 3–1 and 3–2 show the theoretical radii achievable for various thicknesses of hardwood specimens. It must be emphasized that the figures given are rounded up to the nearest whole number and are intended as a helpful guide. Either the radius achievable for a given thickness, or the thickness required for a given radius, should be verified by trials before embarking on a project with limited or precious material. A simple conversion can be used for other sizes if required; for cold bending, 50:1, and for hot bending, 12.5:1.

Tables 3–1 and 3–2 (following page).
The radii that can be achieve used hot
and cold bending on hardwood.

Table 3–1
Cold-Wood Bending

Thickness		Radius	
Inch	Millimeter	Inch	Millimeter
2	50	100	2550
1½	38	75	1915
1	25	50	1275
⅞	22	44	1120
¾	19	33	840
⅝	16	31	790
½	12	25	630
⅜	9	19	485
¼	6	12	306
⅛	3	6	150
1/16	2	3	75

Table 3–2

Hot-Wood Bending

Thickness		Radius	
Inch	**Millimeters**	**Inch**	**Millimeters**
2	50	25	635
1½	38	19	480
1	25	12.5	330
⅞	22	11	280
¾	19	9	230
⅝	16	8	200
½	12	6	150
⅜	9	5	125
¼	6	3	75
⅛	3	1.5	38
¹⁄₁₆	2	¾	20

DRY BENDING

"Dry bending" is a method of bending that uses wood not treated by soaking, heating, steaming, or prepared in any way other than cutting it to a required size.

Assuming that the workpiece is being worked at normal room temperature with moderate moisture content, say about 12 percent, the following information is worth noting. An equation supplied by the Forest Products Research Laboratory is a useful guide when assessing the bending potential of a wooden member. Of course, it would be wise to test some samples before working on precious materials. This is the equation: $T \times R = 0.02$. T is the thickness of the workpiece, R is the radius of the intended curvature. For example, if the workpiece is 1 inch thick and it is necessary to calculate the smallest radius achievable, the formula would be transposed thus: $T \times 0.002 = R$. In this case, since the material is 1 inch thick, the equation would be as follows: $1 \times 0.002 = R$.

There is a simple alternative to the given formula that may have more appeal to those less mathematically secure: to get the radius, multiply the workpiece thickness by 50. To make life even easier, Tables 3–1 and 3–2 show theoretically achievable radii for given thicknesses.

As may be readily seen by this example, even allowing for slight variations in individual workpieces, the achievable bend is relatively small—that is, there is a large radius. Even if this bend is sufficient to suit the job in hand, there remains a fundamental problem: when the force used to create the bend is released, the workpiece will return to its original shape! Well, almost. In some cases, complete recovery can occur. On one occasion, a piece of ebony that was planned for a fingerboard for an instrument had a slight curve in its length. Applying it to the instrument without correcting this would have risked some stressing of adjacent parts, and the piece was too thin to allow planing it to achieve the desired straightness. With several clamps applied to an ebony "sandwich" between two hefty planks, the workpiece was subjected to sufficient pressure to straighten it. After three weeks the clamps were released and the ebony, when examined, revealed no discernible change in its original shape.

It is worth pointing out that it would take considerable effort to achieve a bend of 50 inches radius in a piece of hardwood 1 inch thick, however relatively "slight" it may appear if drawn to scale. Some mechanical aid is advisable if members of this size are to be used. (See chapter 6 for information on using a block and tackle.)

As was mentioned above, even if a bend were produced in the dry material, the piece will return to its previously straight state when the bending force is removed if it has not been fixed in place. As an example, if the workpiece were attached by adhesive to another piece of wood of a similar size, and both were held together on a shaped former, or mold, until set, a laminated shape would be produced. This is discussed in the next section.

LAMINATED BENDING

As was stated earlier, cold, untreated wood may be bent, to a certain extent, without fracturing, particularly if it is in relatively thin strips, say less than ¼ inch thick. Refer to Table 3–1 on page 43 for guidance in this respect. Timber retains its elasticity, however, resulting in its resuming its original shape when the bending force is removed. By attaching the bent member to another adjacent piece shaped similarly to that of the required bend, the curve may be retained. An example would be found in the use of a mold, or form, such as might be used in boat building (3–4 and 3–5). This assumes that the members will become attached together permanently.

It is necessary to clarify the difference between lamination and veneering. In laminations, the layered strips are all arranged with the grain oriented in the same direction. This, without exception, should run with the length,

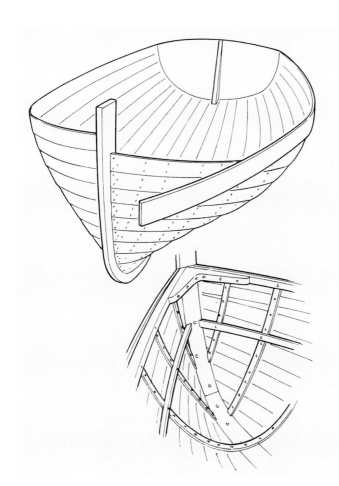

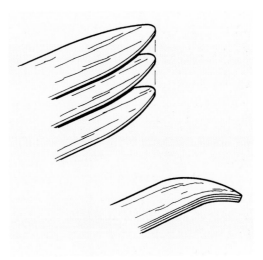

3–4 (left). While not an example of common lamination, this method of attaching boat members is in principle similar in that the planks are laid, while pliant, alongside each other and supported by adjacent planks, the attached ribs, and the stem with clenched nails. They are retained in the form as permanently bent members, it is hoped!

3–5 (below). The method frequently used to produce water skis represents an excellent example of bent lamination. The grain is parallel throughout all the lamina.

as was described in "Bending Characteristics of Wood" on pages 15 to 21.

Veneering differs in that the layers have the grain oriented differently with each alternate layer (3–6). Flexibility is reduced and strength increased in this application, similar in principle to plywood.

Before lamination can proceed, the slats or plies must be produced, the cost of which, in terms of material and production time, might outweigh the value of the item. However, if the design demands lamination, then some thought should be wisely given to structure and material types.

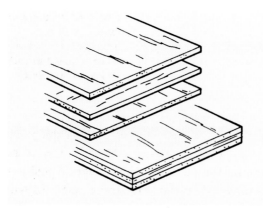

3–6. Normally, plywood and veneered panels are made from gluing an odd number of thin sheets together with the grain of adjacent sheets at right angles to each other.

Some disadvantages with lamination may include high costs due to preparation of slats and the removal of the unsightly glue lines between the slats. Bends may not be possible in compound planes by lamination, and such operations demand more skill and complex equipment.

Benefits, on the other hand, include the possibility of building up extra-thick pieces from more or less any timber, plus the construction of long bent members with no softening treatment needed.

Laminating techniques use thin pieces of wood and, taking the principle further, several pieces may be glued together and then bent against a form and held there until the glue has set. Plies, or the form, should be separated with cling film, a coat of varnish, or a layer of plastic tape, to prevent undesirable adhesion of the laminates and the mold.

A practical solution is provided by this method for the production of larger members by cold bending. Lamination is the term used to describe the uniting of layers of material, whether the same or otherwise. In this method, the layers are called lamina or plies and if made from the same piece of material, with care, they may be reunited in a form made to appear to be from a solid piece. Alternatively, a decorative effect can be produced by using alternate layers of different colors or materials.

Laminating is ideal for the production of comparatively thick members with small radius using almost any species of timber. Even wood of poor quality with faults that would normally be unsuitable for bending might be used for lamination. Long lengths may be laminated due to the possibility of "staggered scarfing" within the lengths of the plies (3–7).

A laminated bend is easier to "set" than one produced by other bending methods due to the adhesive retaining the plies in the shape of the form. Even so, a slight "spring-back" should be anticipated when the laminated member is removed from the restraining effect of the form. As a general principle, the more laminations, the less spring-back, so for a given member it is best to plan for as many plies as may conveniently be prepared. Preparation includes ensuring that the faces to be glued are smooth and the plies of uniform thickness. A table saw should be used to cut the plies to nominal thickness followed by planing of the faces if possible. Without these provisions, unequal pressures will occur, leading to weakness and unsightly glue lines (3–8).

In the interest of successful gluing, it is best if the moisture content is less than 20 percent

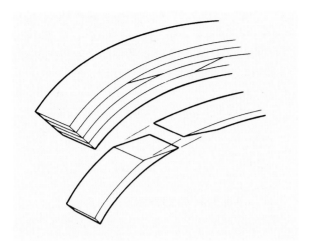

3–7. Scarf joints shown as part of the internal makeup of a laminated assembly.

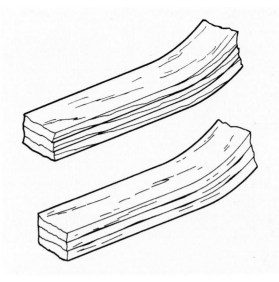

3–8. In the upper example, the glue lines are thin and uniform in thickness, both features desirable in this application. The lower example, however, has uneven glue lines indicating poor preparation of the plies and possible failure of the bend due to lack of uniformity.

for the lamination process. A gap-filling glue is a wise choice for lamination, but it should not be a derivative of polyvinyl acetate (PVA) or aliphatic glues; laminations coated with these glues have a tendency to move gradually after removal from the form. Better to use a urea formaldehyde resin, which sets more slowly but produces a harder, less-discernible glue line with less perceptible movement.

Bearing in mind that each ply must be glued, it is worth applying the adhesive with a paint roller to ensure its uniform thickness and speed of application. It is wise to test-bend the plies on the mold before gluing, to see that their thickness is physically adequate to take the intended curvature.

If a mark is made across the workpiece before it is cut into plies, then it is easy to reassemble the pieces in their original positions to produce a natural grain appearance. As with any other gluing operation, clamping together the members with sufficient and consistent pressure to make them join is fundamental. A satisfactory method is achieved with a two-piece mold between which the plies are clamped (3–9). Practical details are similar to those shown in chapter 6.

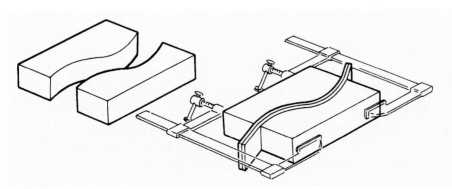

3–9. A straightforward way of producing a bend to secure laminated members.

A point worth remembering in the production of a two-part mold* is that the two parts cannot be produced by simply making one cut with a band saw and separating the shapes. As 3–10 shows, it is necessary to make two molds of different curvature, allowing for the fact that the thickness of the member to be bent has concave and convex faces.

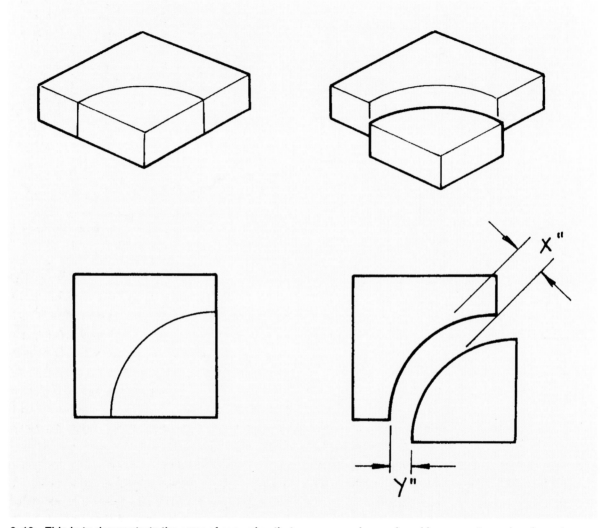

3–10. This is to demonstrate the error of assuming that a curve can be produced by one cut on a band saw to create two parts of a mold. As may be seen, the gap at "X" is greater than that at "Y."

*The words "mold" and "form" are used interchangeably in this and other chapters.

It is possible to cut the curved surfaces of a two-part form simultaneously with a straight cutter mounted in a router (3–11). In this application, the cutter diameter must equal the thickness of the bent member.

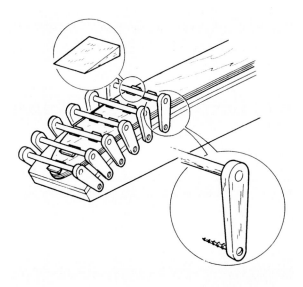

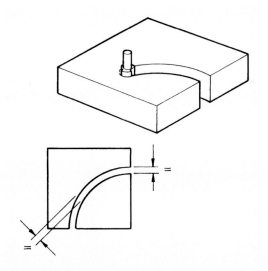

3–12. A ski is the given example of the workpiece being bent on the "swing-and-wedge" jig detailed here.

3–11. Unlike the previous example, here the router cutter produces a gap of uniform thickness in the separation of the two-piece mold.

Sometimes a bent item needs to be duplicated or made in quantity. In such a case, it is probably worth making a jig for the sake of efficiency as well as accuracy. One example is the "swing-and-wedge" jig (3–12). The mold is made up of two sides covered with a flexible top, such as plywood, that is thin enough to follow the curve of the sides. Straddling the mold are the so-called swings. They are made of two small arms connected by a dowel and by screws to the mold sides. There are benefits to making the mold and workpieces match in width; this helps maintain the alignment of the layers due to the swings' containing the sandwich of plies. In practice, the dowels are arranged to leave a gap a little wider than the thickness of the workpiece, the difference being filled with wedges. It is best to work

from the end, progressively adding swings and wedges gradually to produce the bend. This jig is not intended for the rapid techniques associated with hot bending, but it works very well for lamination.

A single-sided form can be used if it has a convex curve; in such a case, a strap is applied to the plies to provide the clamping pressure. This is similar in principle to the method described in chapters 6 and 8.

Molds can be made up of several layers if the required thickness is greater than can be cut by the available resources. A pattern is used to cut each individual layer; these layers are then clamped together, and should probably be glued if they are to be used more than once (3–13). If not, the layers could be separated for some future reuse. If access to a router is available, repetition routing may be used, with conventional template-cutting techniques. These techniques are described in *Router Workshop Bench Reference*, by the author.

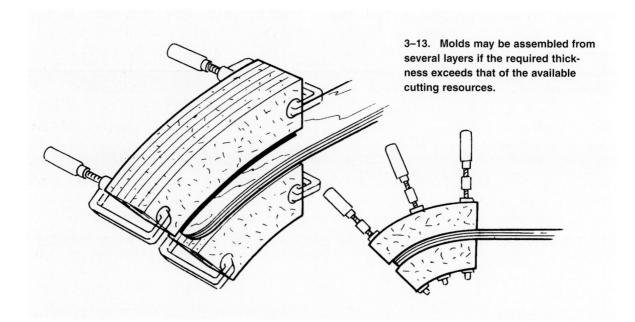

3–13. Molds may be assembled from several layers if the required thickness exceeds that of the available cutting resources.

Clamping between two forms is probably the most straightforward way of deforming the plies, providing the formers are cut correctly. Formers of the same thickness as the workpiece width are practical because they help align the plies. Such applications are best undertaken with four hands, if available.

Whichever type of mold is used to make the lamination, after the adhesive has set completely, the clamps can be removed and the bent members cleaned up. Usually the sides need the most attention, where excess glue and minor discrepancies from irregular alignments of the plies need smoothing. A spokeshave or plane removes major excess, followed by a fine abrasive paper to smooth the surface.

KERF BENDING

When a saw is used to cut wood, the slot made by the saw is known as the "kerf" (3–14). Obviously, a saw blade with a wide set, that is, with its teeth set wide, will make a wide kerf, and a blade with a narrow setting makes a narrow kerf.

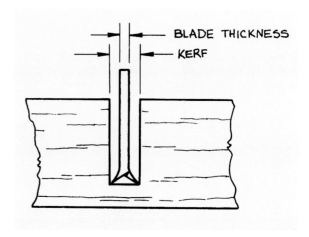

3–14. Here is shown the difference between the thickness of the "cut" and the "kerf."

Choosing the appropriate kerf width is critical when planning a bending process using this method. In basic terms, the member chosen to be bent is almost sawn through its thickness with a series of cuts, in the area where the bend is to be made. The width and spacing of the kerfs is best determined by some tests using waste wood. Effectively, the member is reduced in thickness and may then be bent until the kerfs are closed up. A general guide is not to saw deeper than three-quarters of the thickness of the material and to regard 1/16 inch as the thinnest kerf possible. Thus, by this rule, the thinnest material usable with this method would be 1/4 inch thick. If a kerf needs to be wider than the saw cut, then two or more cuts may be made progressively until the required width of kerf is achieved. This is difficult to produce with uniform cuts by hand sawing, but perfectly feasible with a machine such as a radial arm saw (3–15).

A simple test can be carried out to determine the spacing of kerfs in a particular thickness of wood to produce a required radius. Select a sample workpiece similar to that intended for the project. Make a trial cut to about three-quarters of the thickness of the wood and clamp it on the bench top. Mark off a line equal to the radius from the kerf and raise the free end of the workpiece from the bench top until the kerf is closed. Measure the gap between the bench top to the line drawn for the radius; this should equal the space required between the kerfs to produce a smooth bend (3–16).

As has been stated elsewhere, it is not practicable to bend a piece rectangular in section across the wider part, except that is, with the

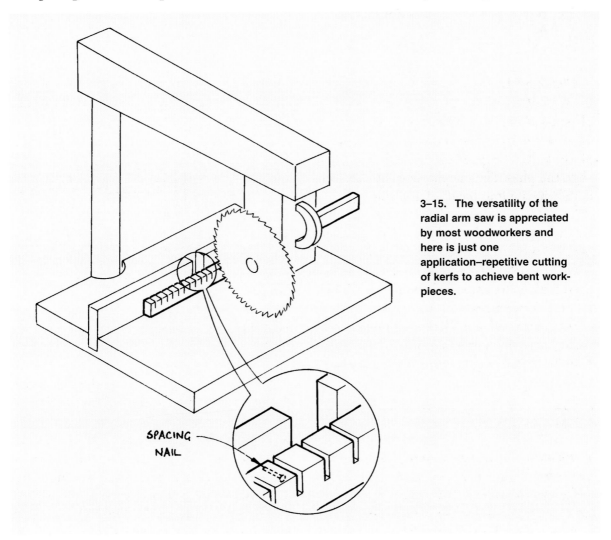

SPACING NAIL

3–15. The versatility of the radial arm saw is appreciated by most woodworkers and here is just one application–repetitive cutting of kerfs to achieve bent work-pieces.

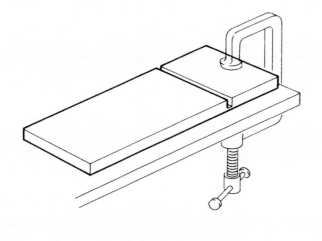

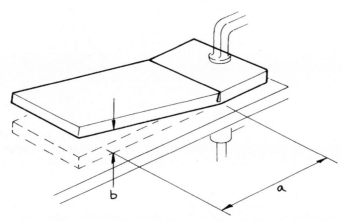

3–16. Here the test piece has been kerfed and clamped to the bench top. There is a mark equal to that of the required radius, and at this point the gap is measured between the test piece and the bench top. This will indicate the distance between the kerfs necessary to achieve the prescribed radius.

kerf method (3–17). Take a workpiece of say, 2 × 1 inches, to be kerfed through its 2-inch width to one-quarter of its thickness. This means that a saw cut 1½ inches deep would leave the recommended ½ inch minimum of material. It will now be clear that the remaining section that will undergo the bending will be ½ × 1 inch across the narrower thickness. Effectively, this will achieve a bend across the wider size of the 2 × 1-inch workpiece.

Several points must be made before embarking upon this very easy bending method:
1. The kerfing method reduces the strength of the material greatly. A little of the strength may be regained if the kerfs are sufficiently narrow

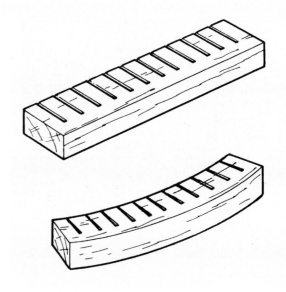

3–17. A rectangular piece can be bent across its wider face by kerfing as shown.

to bring the slotted sides together when the member is bent and a gap-filling glue is used as a binder. Some care is needed to arrange the kerfs correctly.

2. If saw cuts are too close together, there is a risk of breaking away the intervening blocks and causing a local weak spot. An experiment with a similar sized test piece is advised to verify the required spacing of the cuts.

3. In use, the kerfing method is best limited to gap filling and structural reinforcement.

Here are two examples where kerf bending is helpful:

1. Linings for reinforcement at edges of the sides of guitars, violins etc., to add strength and additional gluing area for retaining soundboards and backs (3–18 and 3–19). The sides should already be bent to the finished shape prior to the fitting of the kerfed linings.

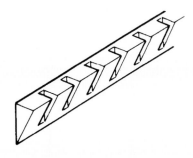 

3–18. In this photograph, the linings are unkerfed. In the lower example may be seen the reinforcement between the ribs and the side. This example may at a glance appear to be kerfed, but further examination will reveal individual blocks, called *tentellones*. The method is found frequently in traditional guitar construction as an excellent reinforcement to the soundboard/rib joint.

3–19. A triangulated section is used for linings for guitars; usually slimmer, rectangular ones are used for violins. Often the linings are fitted before the refinement of the finished section. Note the difference in appearance between the concave and convex bending of the kerfed lining.

2. Coffin sides. At the shoulders of the coffin, the pronounced bend is usually produced by kerfing (3–20). Plywood is often used for coffins due to the combination of strength and economy, since only the outer layer need be of valuable timber. Bending of three-ply boards is straightforward if the kerf runs through two of the plies, because the kerf depth leaves the outer ply uncut and the saw cut is filled with glue.

A variation of the application of kerf bending is one in which the kerfing is orientated along the length of the workpiece rather than across its width (3–21). Effectively, the width of the section to be bent is reduced to that of the material left between the kerfs. These portions may be as little as $\frac{1}{16}$ inch with saw kerfs of say .025 inch. Ideally, the kerf will match the thickness of standard veneer cut into strips for insertion into the kerfs. Left oversize, the veneer strips are inserted and bent at the same time as the main workpiece (3–22). For this operation, a hot-air gun intended for paint stripping may be used (3–23). This gives good local control of heating. See details in "Heating Wood with a Hot-Air Gun and a Jig" on pages 66 to 69. Bending the hot workpiece may be via the double-peg jig as shown in that section.

After the bend is achieved, the veneers are removed, coated with adhesive, and replaced with pressure applied until the adhesive has set (3–24). Trimming any of the waste veneer left protruding from the surface is a simple job with a smoothing block, made from a sheet of abrasive paper wrapped around a piece of wood (3–25).

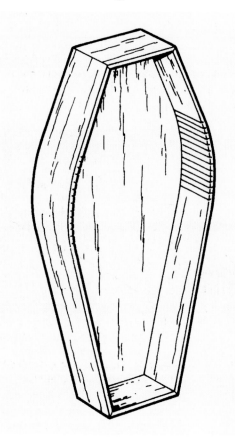

3–20. Kerfing makes possible the smooth curve between the upper and lower coffin sides, achieving at once the use of a plywood case with precious veneer and a sound construction.

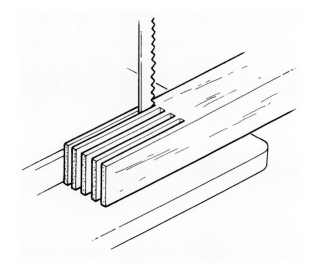

3–21. A workpiece being kerfed along the grain.

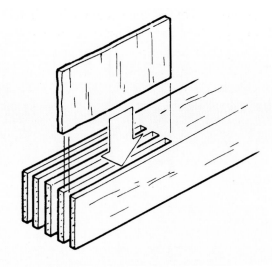

3–22. Veneer strips will be inserted provisionally into the kerf slots.

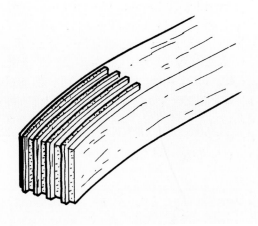

3–24. After bending the workpiece, the veneers are removed, glued, reinserted into the kerf slots, and clamped until dry.

3–23. Heat is applied to the workpiece complete with its inserted, but unglued, veneers.

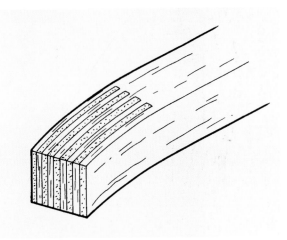

3–25. Excess veneer protruding from the assembly is removed and the workpiece smoothed all round.

Chapter 4

WOOD-HEATING TECHNIQUES

PREPARING BENDS WITH HOT WATER

Techniques for bending wood after immersion in hot water are the same as used for wood heated by steaming. The only difference is in the heating process.

Heating wood by either steaming or boiling makes little difference to the actual bending operation. No advantages to the process are found in heating to a higher temperature than that of boiling water, nor for a period of immersion longer than 45 to 60 minutes per inch of thickness. However, there are certain subjective attitudes that come into play when contemplating heating wood, and this writer is one of those who prefer not to boil. It is with regard to parts for musical instruments that this observation is made. After having carefully seasoned the selected wood, maintained its moisture content in a controlled environment, and then prepared its thickness and surface to specific requirements, the act of plunging it into boiling water seems very unwholesome. In any case, dry heat may be applied to shape most of the bent components for guitars and similar instruments. More details are given in chapter 5. Some craftsmen are more pragmatic and concerned with getting results quickly and easily; boiling is one of them.

Despite the aesthetic appraisal of boiling versus steaming, it is true to say that some advantages accompany the former, particularly in the case of slender pieces. They are:

1. It is easier and quicker to boil water than to produce and control steam.

2. Any metal container of convenient size with a source of heating can suffice. Steam needs a specially constructed chamber, or the acquisition of a suitable alternative such as a pipe (4–1).

3. Boiling is more suitable than steaming for localized heating, such as the ends of sticks (4–2).

4. Normal domestic equipment may be used

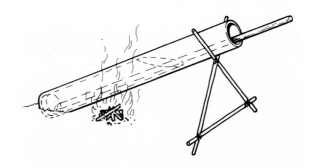

4–1. A simple metal pipe supported over a fire was a common way to heat water for workpieces in rustic settings.

4–2. Ends of sticks or thin members are suitable for heating in a boiling urn.

for boiling; for instance, a kitchen stove and saucepan are very practical (4–3).

Any leak-proof metal container will serve as a boiler if its dimensions are sufficient. For example, a two-gallon oilcan with the top removed works well, being more than deep

4–3. For small items, a domestic saucepan of boiling water is ideal.

enough to cover the required 12 inches of handle, if bending a walking stick, for example. Fastidious cleansing of the interior is essential to ensure that no traces of oil or other contaminant remain before adding the water. Liquids used for the washing of domestic utensils will work well combined with plenty of water for a final rinsing of the oilcan.

A gas or electric heater is adequate for heating the water if the equipment is to be set up outside or in a workshop. With caution in mind, electricity and water being dangerously incompatible, gas is probably the best choice as a heating medium. This can be provided by a portable gas ring connected to a gas line or by portable gas canisters of the type used for camping. Boilers with built-in heaters are fine, being self-contained and deep enough for heating the ends of sticks.

Alternatively, a large cooking pot heated on a domestic stove will do very well, provided that other members of the household are agreeable to the idea! A practical disadvantage to heating in the kitchen is that it is usually not possible to set up the bending equipment nearby.

About 25 minutes insertion is enough boiling to soften the average stick for bending, but again it must be stressed that individual materials have their own characteristics and experimentation with dispensable pieces is advised.

For local heating of small items or the ends of sticks, for example, one of the easiest means of combining hot water and the workpiece is to use a kettle and a bucket. Boiling water can be poured from the kettle down the stick to heat it. A thicker piece may need two kettles applied one following the other. This can be achieved efficiently providing both kettles are boiling at the commencement of the operation. With care, practically the entire workpiece can be heated with this method (4–4).

4–4. **With careful control, a kettle may be used to pour boiling water over a member. If contained in a bucket, the item can be held for a time in the hot water to prolong the contact.**

While on the subject of practicality, it is worth pointing out that a traditional technique used by walking-stick makers of old was to add water to sand and increase the temperature with a fire-burning timber scrap. The ends of the sticks were inserted into the hot, wet sand, where they remained until ready for bending (4–5).

One of the problems associated with all bending operations is that the source of heating and the bending apparatus must be as close together as possible. This is to reduce heat loss to a minimum when the workpiece is removed from the heat. As has been mentioned elsewhere, a test piece used to test the system is a wise precaution. If the test-piece collapses under the effort of bending, it is

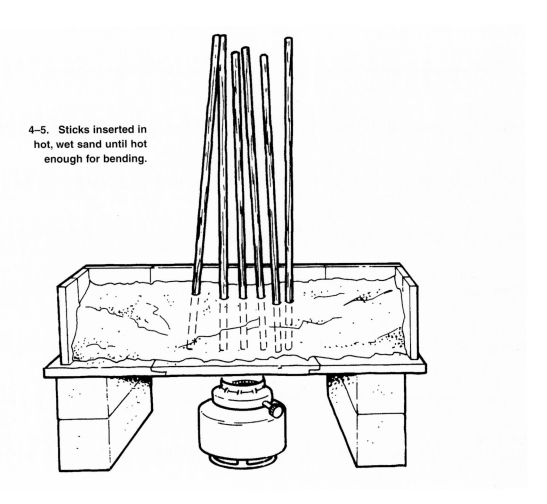

4–5. Sticks inserted in hot, wet sand until hot enough for bending.

probably overheated; if it cracks during the bending, it may need more heat or a longer heating period.

PREPARING BENDS WITH STEAM

Steaming wood, as a preparation for bending it, is one of the most common techniques used in the production of walking sticks, chair backs, boat ribs, and similar items. There are several factors contributing to its popularity, one of the main ones being that it is fairly easy to fill a box with steam. Boiling, as an alternative, requires a container of the equivalent size of the item being bent and, if the items are large, main-taining a sufficient volume of water at boiling point for any length of time is far from easy. Such a process is potentially more hazardous and relatively costly. Although boiling has its adherents and advantages as described in the previous section, in most cases the boiling process is better confined to comparatively lightweight workpieces.

Some may be surprised to learn that the purpose of steaming is not to saturate the solid material with steam, but to heat it and the moisture contained within it to soften the fibers. Moisture content of 25 to 30 percent is best for bending, achievable by steaming to about the boiling point for three-quarters of an hour per inch of thickness, regardless of the width. About two minutes per millimeter is the metric equivalent.

Although it is usual to refer to the whole operation as "steam bending," the process is divided into two parts: first, the generation of steam, and second, containing it. Steam generation is a simple matter, merely needing the application of heat to water. The volume of steam is a question of how much water is being heated and how much heat is being applied. Obviously, a large vessel takes longer to boil for steam generation, uses more applied heat, and is probably more difficult to manage.

Steam may be generated in a kettle (4–6), a tea urn (refer to chapter 11), or by a wallpaper steamer (refer to chapter 10). As long as the boiling water can be maintained without drying out and the generated steam can be ducted efficiently, it matters little which method is used.

Ducting the steam and containing it are additional problems. It is necessary to maintain the high humidity during the steaming process to prevent the wood from drying out. In order to achieve this, the wood must be enclosed in a steam box connected to a steam supply. An essential consideration is the replenishing of water to the boiler. The container must not be allowed to boil dry; if it should, the safest thing is to wait until it is cool and then refill it. Adding cold water to a hot, empty container risks an explosion, likely not only to damage the apparatus but also to cause personal injury. Bob Forsyth, an experienced ship surveyor who lectures on boat building, designed an excellent steam boiler with a built-in, low-water alarm (4–7). A tube is fitted into the lid of the boiler by welding and is suspended above the bottom. When the water level drops below the tube, steam is emitted and blows a whistle fitted to the open end of the tube. Simple, but effective and safe. It makes sense to add hot, rather than cold, water to the container when refilling to help maintain a constant steam generation.

With simplicity in mind, Veritas produces a kettle with an appropriate spout, such as the one supplied with its bending kit. This is easily attached to a plastic-pipe "steam-box" arrangement for small steaming jobs (4–8). As an example, the kettle holds about 3 pints and takes about 8 minutes to come to the boil. During one test run, it ran for 1 hour, 15 minutes and consumed only 1½ pints of water! Subse-

4–6. Direct application of steam from a kettle spout onto the workpiece is just about as basic as it gets, but nonetheless effective on thin sections.

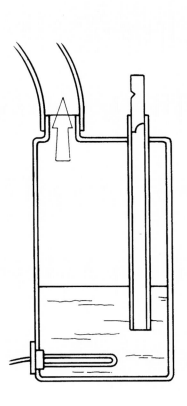

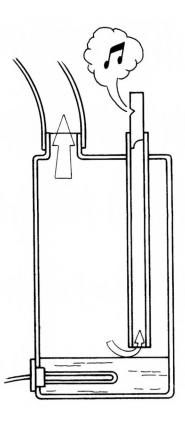

4–7. When steam is generated in the steamer, it is forced out of the hole in the top and is ducted from the container through the pipe. When the level of water drops to lower than the safety pipe, steam enters it and blows the whistle to warn of the need to fill up the container with water. Replenishment is best done with hot water for safety and also to avoid a pause in steam generation.

quently, it has been required to steam for less than an hour for bending sessions, and these jobs it has accomplished without failure of any kind. As may be seen in the illustrations, it also fills the steam box used for most of the examples featured in this book.

This brings us to the subject of the steam box. In principle, the box must be of a size to accommodate the workpieces (4–9). Normally, more than one workpiece is involved with any given bending session, especially considering the need for trial runs with inferior samples.

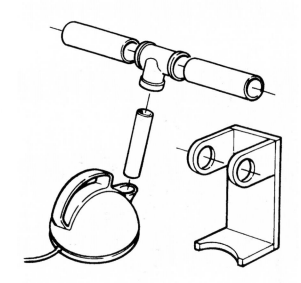

4–8. By adding a T-shaped joint with tube extensions, the kettle may be converted into a small steaming chamber. For safety's sake, a simple stand should be fashioned to secure the tubing while it is generating steam.

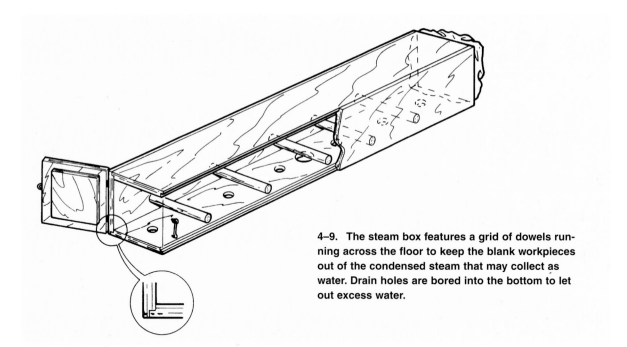

4–9. The steam box features a grid of dowels running across the floor to keep the blank workpieces out of the condensed steam that may collect as water. Drain holes are bored into the bottom to let out excess water.

For obvious reasons, it is best to plan ahead to accommodate as complete a program of bending as possible. Therefore, allowing room between the workpieces for the circulation of the steam, the basics of the design of the box may be determined (4–10). Bear in mind that bigger pieces might be needed in future projects, so maybe a margin of extra space might be allowed.

Material for the construction of the steam box can consist of solid wood or an exterior-grade plywood (4–11 and 4–12). Particleboard is not recommended, due to its tendency to decompose when in contact with water. Corners should be half-jointed or grooved for strength and to help to prevent the escape of steam. Glue should not be necessary if the joints are secure, but it is prudent to add a compound such as that used in heating systems to ensure a good seal. Screws are used rather than nails to secure the parts of the box. If possible, the screws should be treated with a surface coat-

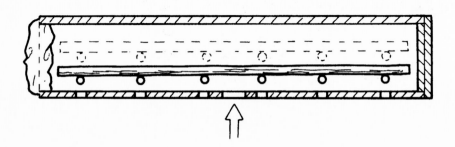

4–10. A section view of the steam box shows how another horizontal row of dowel may be added above the lower one, to provide an extra layer of workpieces if required. The central hole in the floor of the box is for the entry of the steam pipe.

ing, such as galvanizing, to protect from corrosion and eventual failure.

A hole of suitable diameter to admit the steam pipe must be bored into the bottom of the box. If the pipe from the steam generator, be it kettle, urn, or whatever, is metal, then a stout hose, such as that used for car radiators, is suitable for the link to the steam box. The flexibility of the hose should allow manipulation for ease of handling and fitting. As the steam source logically will be beneath the steam box, it follows that the latter will need to be suspended above the ground. A simple answer is to stand the steam box on a couple of boxes at a height appropriate to clear the steam source (4–13). One bonus in using this system is that it makes

4–11. The dowels used on this steam box were made from an old broomstick; their ends were split with a saw to admit wedges. A coating of sealant for heating systems was given to the ends of the dowels before they were inserted into the holes. As shown here, tapered wedges were hammered into the slots to expand the dowels, ensuring a steam-proof seal.

4–12. Wedges were made overlong and trimmed after being hammered home.

it easier to load and unload the workpieces.

One end of the box is usually stuffed with a wad of cloth to prevent the escape of steam (4–14). This is an imperfect seal, intentionally so because the steam must not be allowed to become pressurized, for reasons of safety. However, this wad works, not only as a seal but also as an adjustable box end. If short pieces are to be steamed, the wad is simply pushed inside the steam box to reduce its length accordingly.

A more refined steam box may be constructed by making two boxes, one made to slide inside the other; this permits adjustment to the length of the chamber (4–15). Remembering the potential for distortion of wood when

4–13. Sturdy trestles were made to support the box at the correct working height above the kettle; a piece of rubber hose joins the two trestles.

4–14. A wad of waste cloth is used to seal the end of the box to prevent the escape of steam. In practice, a small amount of steam filters gently through the cloth, but this also acts as a safety valve preventing any possibility of building up dangerous steam pressure.

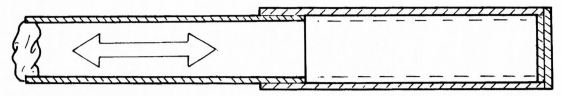

4–15. To allow for the use of workpieces of differing lengths, a two-box system can be made. This is a "box inside-a-box," one being small enough to slide into the other. A close fit is required, but not so close that adjustment is prevented.

heated, it is best if the difference in the sizes of the two boxes is enough to prevent binding.

A hinged trap door with a catch to secure it completes the requirements for the steam box, except to say that if it is to be operated outside or in a cold environment, a blanket may be spread over the box for extra insulation. In this case, precaution must be taken to see that the blanket is not in contact with, or near any source of, heat that could ignite it.

Before loading the workpieces, it is essential that the steam box be heated and full of steam. To verify this, the box top should be hot to the touch and opening the door briefly will allow a slight escape of steam. If the workpieces are loaded before reaching working temperature, the effect is to dry out the wood before it is steamed properly; this can make it brittle.

Loading and unloading must be efficient and rapid, to avoid the loss of steam from the box and the loss of heat from the item to be bent when removing it for the bending process (4–16). In other words, not only must the steam production and bending system be adequate but the handling of the workpiece between operations must be efficient. Gloves should be worn to facilitate the safe removal of the hot workpieces, and the distance between the steam box and the bending equipment reduced to a minimum.

4–16. Loading is quick and efficient with the hinged trap door fitting well and fitted with a hook to secure it.

HEATING WOOD WITH A HOT-AIR GUN AND A JIG

This method of heating wood requires the use of a hot-air gun. Originally designed for softening paint and varnish as an aid to stripping, this appliance is ideal for the production and direction of controlled heat. It can be used in a similar manner to a flashlight. By aiming it at a particular area, heat can be directed similar to the way one aims a beam of light. It is worth adding that since the gun delivers a beam hot enough to melt varnish, it is potentially dangerous and can cause serious personal injury if operated without care.

Heat penetration can be controlled, up to a point, by two factors: by adjusting the distance at which the gun is held from the workpiece and by regulating how long the heat is applied. This is assuming the particular heat gun is not fitted with the facility to control the heat output.

At its best, this method is used for the heating of thin workpieces, such as slats for trugs (gardening baskets), sides for guitars and violins, etc. Due to the random spread of heat from the nozzle of the gun, care should be taken when holding short pieces in front of it.

Bearing in mind that thin workpieces not only heat up very quickly, they also cool down very quickly, ideally the mold, form, or other element involved in the bending setup should be arranged close to the heating process. Portability of the gun allows this conveniently.

It is worth considering the possibility of holding the gun in a clamp of some sort, to allow a two-handed hold on the workpiece. This may have advantages in the reduction of handling time, allowing continuity of movement of the workpiece from the heating process to its application on the form.

This method of heating works well with the double-peg jig described and illustrated in this section. The jig is easily made from cutoffs or spare boards. The jig shown in the illustrations is made of scrap medium-density fiberboard and a piece of broomstick.

In principle, the jig works by placing a "cold" (unheated) portion of the workpiece to be held between two pegs, while the heated portion is bent to the required radius. A wide variety of geometrically related positions may be arranged with the pegs inserted in the radially distributed holes. During the bending operation, if the workpiece cools down before the required radius is achieved heat is directed by the hot-air gun to the precise location where needed.

Illus. 4–17 shows the details for the jig used in hot-air bending. Illus. 4–18 to 4–25 show hot-air bending applications and the types of items that can be built using this approach.

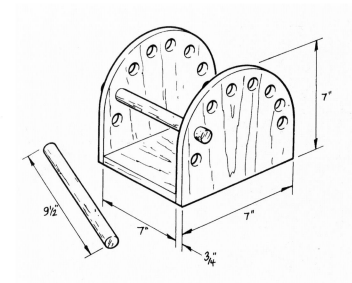

4–17. Dimensions of the double-peg jig are relative to the sizes of workpieces and should be adjusted accordingly. Holes for the dowels should be large enough to make insertion and removal easy and unrestricted.

4–18. All that is needed for the hot-air setup, for heating and bending. The hot-air gun is one of the cheapest available with many years of active service as a paint stripper. The jig was made from cutoffs and the pegs from an old broomstick.

4–19. The slat being bent has been trapped between the base and the jig. In this application, only one peg is used. Heat is applied to soften the workpiece until it yields to the lifting pressure exerted by the hand.

4–20. A similar application, but with the workpiece trapped between two pegs while being heated in the same way.

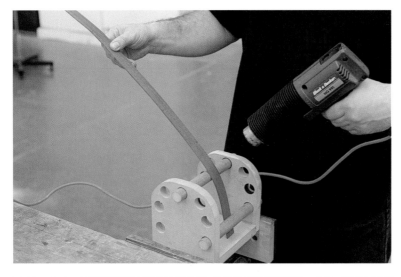

4–21. In this case, the pegs are separated by four holes, spreading the points of contact wider apart.

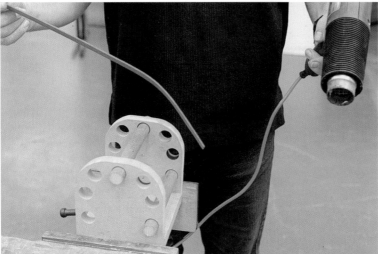

4–22. A slight bend that has been removed from the jig to allow it to cool. It will now be set at that angle permanently. As always, some allowance should be made for a slight spring-back in time if the workpiece is left unsupported.

4–23. Here a wider workpiece similar to a guitar rib is being heated and bent, with two pegs set five holes apart. Good control and a wide range of angles and bent shapes are possible with this method.

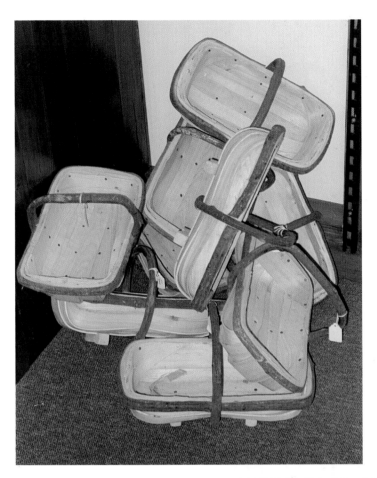

4–24 and 4–25. The slats used to make these gardening baskets could be heated by the hot-air method described here. The handle and edge trim could be bent with hot water or steam preparation.

4–25.

Chapter 5

HOT-PIPE BENDING

Most stringed instruments have a hollow body, or sound chamber, that amplifies the sound of the activated string. Often as not, the sides, usually called ribs, are curved to make the characteristic shape of the particular instrument. Although many instruments are similar, few are identical. Taking for example the violin family, which includes violins, violas, cello, and double bass, the obvious difference is the size, yet if they were all brought to a similar size by scaling, they would differ in other more subtle ways. The same applies to the viols, the ancient relatives of the violins. As for guitars, given that they all have a waisted section a little above halfway along the length of the body, variations of length, width, and depth are endless. Whether the ribs of the instrument are made from a composite of several pieces or from one piece has an effect on the method of construction, but the principles of bending the parts will be similar.

Although there are excellent examples of mass-produced instruments, there are also vast quantities produced singly by amateurs and professional luthiers all over the world. For these producers, one of the major advantages of hot-pipe bending is that individual shapes are obtainable boundlessly and none need ever be duplicated unless desired.

Bending wood on a hot pipe differs from most other bending processes in that both the heating and bending are achieved at virtually the same time. When steam, hot water, or hot air is used to heat the workpiece, the softened wood is bent by applying it to a mold or former. It is acknowledged that these methods are used by some luthiers for the production of instrument sides (ribs); nevertheless, they are so few as to be disregarded as far as this book is concerned. Without doubt, the majority of luthiers use a hot-pipe process, and it is with this in mind that the following applies.

Using hand manipulation of wood on a hot pipe is a demanding affair requiring some prerequisites without which the process could easily fail.

Hot-pipe bending is suitable for relatively thin workpieces, say, between ³⁄₆₄ths and ³⁄₁₆ths of an inch thick, with widths of up to about 6 inches. Preparing a workpiece of uniform thickness is essential because when the workpiece is applied to the heated iron, if there is any inconsistency in the mass of the material, control is more difficult to maintain (5–1). A portion that is thinner than normal will bend more readily and unexpectedly, resulting in overbending at that point. In this case, by reversing the workpiece it is possible to adjust the bend to recover the correct shape. While this may be unavoidable, it is undesirable because there is the distinct possibility that the surface will become uneven, lacking the smooth flowing lines associated with musical instruments.

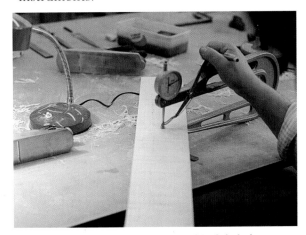

5–1. **Prior to bending this guitar side, it is being checked with a gauge to ensure that the thickness is uniform throughout the workpiece.**

In the case of musical instruments, the material type is usually prescribed by tradition and occasionally by fashion. For example, high-quality backs and sides of violins are expected to be made in sycamore or maple and guitars in rosewood, although, happily, there are some exceptions. Straight-grained species are the most obliging to the bender, particularly if the grain runs straight along the whole length of the workpiece. Extra length—as much as 1½ inches—is allowed at each end of the workpiece, to allow for the possibility of shakes (splits) developing. This can happen despite the greatest care being taken, and close examination of the ends and the entire surface of the workpiece is advised before commencing the bending operation. Any flaw should be regarded as a potential hazard and the piece should be set aside.

As to the hot pipe itself; it is probably so called because the early wood-bending technicians used the hot chimney attached to the stove; however, any pipe capable of being heated and maintaining its temperature for the duration of the bending process would suffice. Achieving the desirable temperature, assuming this is known, and controlling it, is the predominant requirement of the hot-pipe system. It must not be forgotten that its shape, be it a circular or an oval section, must be small enough to produce the required radius of bend in the workpiece.

Let's consider first the material of the hot pipe itself. This may be the simplest tube made of heavy-section metal (say, of 2 inches internal diameter with a wall thickness of ¼ inch) that would lend itself to being preheated by open fire, gas flame, or an electric heat source. Providing the bending process can be accomplished without delay, it is likely that the pipe will retain sufficient heat to achieve the required bend. If not, then of course the pipe would be returned to the heat source in order to continue the operation. There are some inconvenient obstacles to overcome in this method, and it will not be detailed here.

A pipe with its own internal heat source (such as a so-called bending iron), usually heated by an electric element, is a convenient tool that is easily operated and readily available from luthiers' suppliers. Such a tool is thermostatically controlled with a rotary knob marked to indicate the temperature. It takes up little space in storage and is easily set up with few problems of operation (5–2). Usually, the purchased bending iron has an oval cross-section with asymmetrical radii at each end. As to cost, electric irons vary, but one might dine for a week on the current average price. This writer's own preference is a self-made pipe, made from a cylinder liner from a diesel engine, obtained from a junkyard, that is heated with a gas firelighter bought at a garage sale. It costs about as much as a modest bottle of wine.

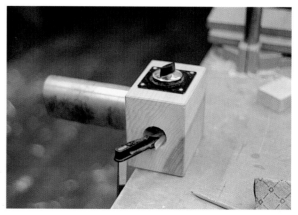

5–2. An electric bending iron is clamped to the bench top, set up in horizontal mode.

Before describing the application of a conventional electric bending iron, a description of the gas-heated pipe with some of its virtues is warranted. A steel tube about 3 inches in diameter and about 10 inches long is the "pipe." It sits on four short legs fixed to a baseboard that keeps the assembly rigid when clamped in a horizontal position to the workbench. A gas poker of the type used to light fireplaces functions with propane gas through a rubber connection to a portable gas cylinder (5–3 and 5–4).

5–3. The author's hot pipe after much successful use in the production of ribs for guitars, lutes, dulcimeters, gitterns, and other stringed instruments.

fixed horizontally and resting firmly on its legs, there is no danger of loosening its fittings during the application of pressure to achieve the bending of the workpiece.

On the other hand, the electric bending iron, since it is fixed at its bottom end, whether it is used in the vertical or horizontal position, is subjected to a cantilever force. Often this results in loosening of the base fixing, leading to other mechanical and electrical complications.

If water is used in the bending process, there is clearly a danger if a damp or dripping workpiece is brought to the electric bending iron, due to the incompatibility of electricity

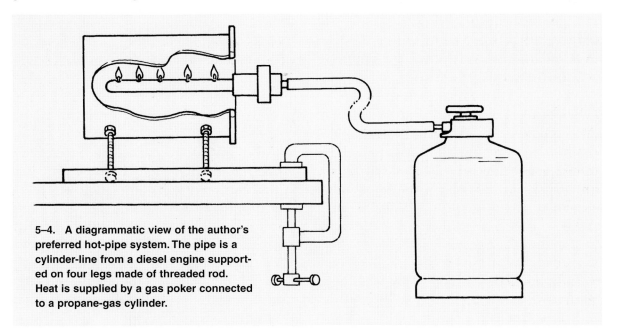

5–4. A diagrammatic view of the author's preferred hot-pipe system. The pipe is a cylinder-line from a diesel engine supported on four legs made of threaded rod. Heat is supplied by a gas poker connected to a propane-gas cylinder.

Among the advantages of this equipment over its electric competitor is that initially it takes much less time to set this up (from removing it from its storage box to achieving operating temperature) than it does to heat up the electric bending iron for use. Also, due to the relatively thin walls of the tube, adjustment of the temperature, up or down, is rapid and achieved by adjusting the flow of gas by the control knob on the gas cylinder. Because it is

and water. This does not apply to the gas-heated pipe, of course; in fact, a damp cloth may be placed on the pipe and left as a wet cushion to help the operation. Many experienced luthiers prefer to work like this with a wet-cloth "sandwich" or with presoaked wood. Wet cloth between the pipe and the workpiece allows its moisture to turn to steam, helping to drive the heat through the wood. It also ensures that the workpiece is protected from scorching, because the cloth will dry out and burn first and thus give a timely warning of the potential danger of overheating.

It is worth a short review of this question of whether or not to use water in the bending of the sides of musical instruments. Arguably the most prolific producers of traditional guitars are the Spanish makers. They did invent the instrument, after all. In the workshops of the master builders in Spain, the majority use dry woods with no preliminary soaking or wetting during the bending operation. It has been mentioned elsewhere that steam or hot water are only a means of heating through the whole thickness of the workpiece; heat itself is the key to softening the wood and not water, cold or hot. Nevertheless, as stated above, the wet-cloth sandwich is a very practical way of heating without danger of scorching.

Assuming the wood has been correctly prepared to the correct thickness, the iron, of whichever type, is set up securely. The pattern to which the workpiece is to be bent should be set up nearby for easy reference. To help determine the correct temperature for the chosen workpiece, it will help if a test piece is available of the same material. Begin by dripping water onto the hot iron. If the drops sit sizzling on the iron, it probably means that the temperature is not high enough. If the drops of water are flung off or evaporate instantly on contact with the hot surface, it may be too hot. So try to judge somewhere in between. It must be emphasized that there is no hard and fast rule about this and even if an accurate thermometer were incorporated in the system, different materials and thicknesses would demand different treatment.

Practical indications of correct heat levels will be found in applying the workpiece to the iron. For instance, if the wood begins to scorch before the bend is achieved, the iron is too high. Alternatively, if the wood is stubborn, re-quiring much pressure with little bending achieved, the iron is not hot enough. As always, experience is required to accomplish the task with any degree of assured success; hence, the need for some test pieces.

Consider a guitar rib as an example of several radii connected by a smooth-flowing series of curves. It is necessary to determine whether to begin at the waist, that is, more or less in the center of the workpiece, and work toward each end, or to work from one end to the other. Excellent examples of each method may be used by different luthiers, with probably a majority starting from the waist. It matters little which is used, but in the case of the "waist first" approach, the center of the waist radius must be marked accurately on each blank and on the appropriate face. This is to ensure that the sides will be bent symmetrically and that the process provides a pair and not two left-hand, or two right-hand sides!

Measuring around the pattern with a piece of string will ascertain where the waist will be located (5–5); don't forget to add a little extra on the end for safety, for trimming back later.

Taking the electric bending iron as the most common tool, the procedure for bending a guitar rib is as follows. Assume that the workpiece is a straight-grained rosewood of about ⅛th inch thick, about 4 inches wide, and about 35 inches long. It is one of a pair and it will be bent from the waist first without wetting or soaking.

Holding the rib in both hands, one at each end, and pressing the "waist" against the iron, be sure that the bottom edge of the rib is resting on the table of the iron. This is to make sure that the bend will be square to the edge and not at some tangent that might cause a twist in the rib.

Local heating with cold areas on either side of the contact with the iron might lead to rupturing of the outer surface fibers if pressure is applied. To avoid this, a rocking action is pro-

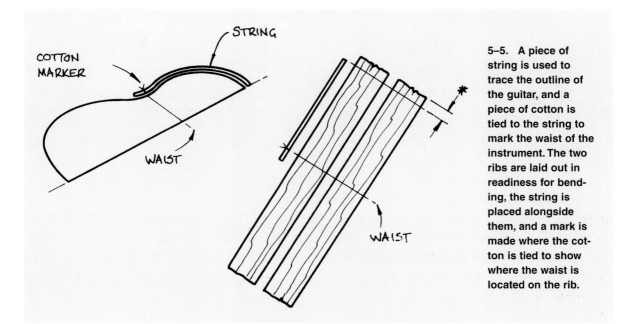

5–5. A piece of string is used to trace the outline of the guitar, and a piece of cotton is tied to the string to mark the waist of the instrument. The two ribs are laid out in readiness for bending, the string is placed alongside them, and a mark is made where the cotton is tied to show where the waist is located on the rib.

duced to make a wider contact with the iron and spread the heat to either side of the pressure point (5–6). This helps to keep the material flexible and less likely to crack. On no account should this be attempted by sliding the wood to-and-fro across the iron. This action would literally "iron" the face of the wood, leading to its hardening and possible cracking of the surface fibers.

It is possible to feel the wood begin to plasticize after a few moments' contact with the heated iron until the material begins to yield under pressure from the hands. At this point, some attention must be paid to the amount of bend and the radius being produced. Frequent reference to the pattern must be made to determine to what degree the bend is to be progressed (5–7 to 5–10).

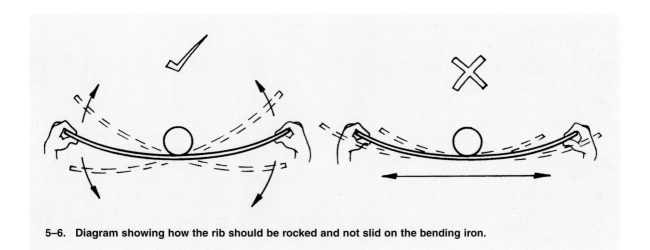

5–6. Diagram showing how the rib should be rocked and not slid on the bending iron.

5–7. Producing the first bend, that is, the waist of the guitar rib. The bending iron is set in vertical mode for this operation. Individual preferences apply; the iron could be clamped horizontally.

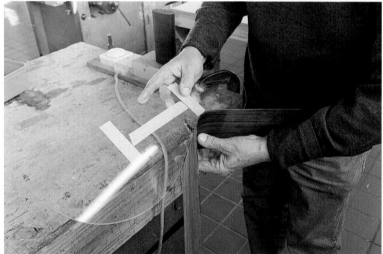

5–8. Comparing the bent workpiece with the pattern. Often as not, frequent checks and adjustments are necessary to achieve an acceptable fit.

5–9. As one looks at a guitar body, it has a wide part at the top and bottom with a "waist" in between. The wider parts are called "bouts," upper and lower respectively. As shown here, a progression has been made to curves for the upper bout, that is, the last bend to complete the rib; extra care is needed at this point to avoid minor errors.

5–10. Nearly there. Another gentle application to the iron and the rib bending is finished. All that is needed then is another rib to match it exactly!

When the final shape is achieved, the second rib is bent and fixed temporarily by tape to its twin (5–11). Both are left to cool and, hopefully, set to the required shape. It is best to attach the ribs to the soundboard of the guitar as quickly as possible, even while still warm if in time, the better to achieve the final shape. Illus. 3–19 on page 53 shows two guitar bodies without their backs to illustrate bent ribs and attached linings.

HOT-PIPE BENDING VIOL RIBS

With reference to the bending of the guitar rib in the foregoing, the same suggestions apply equally to the bending of ribs for the violin family, including the viola, cello, double bass, and all varieties of viol. Some exceptions are worth noting, however; the ribs for this category of instrument are made up of multiple sections,

5–11. Both ribs when matched to the pattern are fixed together by a low-tack tape, until they are built into the instrument. Keeping them together, like a lamination, in the meantime helps to prevent spring-back.

usually three per side. This differs from the guitar, which has a one-piece rib on each side.

In 5–12 to 5–16, Jane Julier, one of the most highly respected luthiers in the world, specializing in the viol, demonstrates the hot-pipe bending of voil ribs.

5–12. One of the pieces to make up a viol rib in the first stages of bending. The material is sycamore with an attractive figure.

5–13. Testing the partially formed rib against a finished example to achieve an accurate duplicate.

5–14. Working close to the end of the rib portion is difficult to manage without risk of burned fingers, so a metal strap is used. This also helps to prevent undesirable breakout of fibers on the outside of the bend.

5–15. Viewed from this angle, the strap hides the workpiece completely and the hands are safely away from contact with the hot iron.

5–16. A completed set of ribs attached to the mold temporarily, but fixed permanently to the blocks seen at each end of the assembly. Later when the adhesives have set, the soundboard will be fitted.

Viol with a Five-Piece Soundboard

In the case of the viol, one type in particular, though not unique, is an English model that features a five-piece soundboard. This curved and arched member is usually carved from solid spruce, whereas in the case of the five-piece version it is bent and then carved. Obviously the reason for bending to shape is to reduce the amount of material used and the time taken in carving. There is also the possibility that in principle, the grain, being bent to the required shape, may respond better to and conduct vibrations more easily than the grain on the viol carved from solid wood. Here one may recollect the advantage of the grown knee versus the knee sawn from solid wood (refer to "Why Bend Wood?" on page 15). In 5–17 to 5–24 Jane Julier demonstrates a process that requires skill and experience beyond that of a beginner.

5–17. On the left is a completed soundboard for a viol, made in the five-piece principle; alongside are the five pieces that are to be bent and joined for a duplicate.

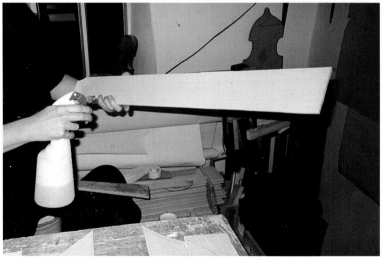

5–18. A splash of water to help prevent scorching of the workpiece. As was mentioned elsewhere, softwood, such as this spruce, is more difficult to bend than hardwood, necessitating more contact with the hot iron.

5–19. Considerable pressure is needed to deform the spruce, as may be seen in the application of the rib to the iron set up in horizontal mode for that purpose.

5–20. Just a small part of the work-piece is being applied to the heat to bring about a refinement of arch to suit that particular portion of the soundboard.

5–21. Some of the pieces are complex with twists and compound curves, demanding great strength and subtle control combined with awareness of the workpiece as a three-dimensional object. Jane's skills as a wood carver serve her well in this respect.

5–22.   Having bent the five pieces to the required shape, it is now necessary to plane the edges meticulously to produce perfect edge-to-edge joints. Any minuscule error at this point can render the instrument partially mute and prone to undesirable buzzes.

5–23.   All the pieces have been married into one and the surfaces, inside and out, have been smoothed to establish a nominal thickness. Some refinement will likely be forthcoming after the soundboard is fitted to the body of the instrument.

5–24.   A unique viol fashioned by Jane Julier, in all its elegant splendor.

Chapter 6

BENDING WITH CLAMPS AND MOLD

Bending jigs frequently have similar components and, as with other projects, equipment is the better for being limited to as few items as possible. Clamps of almost any kind may be used, with the advantage of quick-release or quick-action types being preferred, especially for hot-bending operations. As to the mold*, this may be defined as any frame or shape used for reference, or against which a softened material may be laid in order to change its shape. Generally, it is made of inferior wood or particleboard.

A ONE-SIDED MOLD

A simple example would be used for a slightly bent item made from a thin section, say ¼-inch-thick material bent while hot to about a 12-inch radius. A one-sided mold could be cut from particleboard and notched to seat C-clamps (6–1). A test should be performed on a spare blank to ensure the material will accept the bend without rupturing, With no strap to bind the workpiece to the shape, there is always the attendant danger of failure in this type of application if too small a radius is attempted (see chapter 7 for additional information).

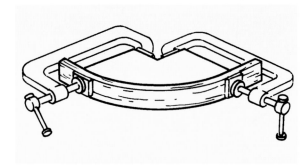

6–1.   A one-sided mold could be cut from particleboard and notched to seat C-clamps.

MOLDING AN "S" BEND

A more complex example using an "S" shape applies clamp-and-mold principles. Made from blockboard, the mold is in two parts with the intention of compressing several workpieces simultaneously (6–2). Both parts of the mold are cut from one piece, the curve being smooth and symmetrical.

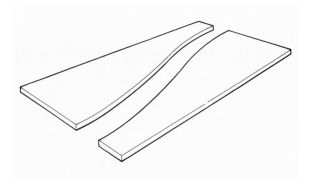

6–2.   Two parts make up the mold, which is cut from blockboard.

In the following example, two sizes of workpiece from kiln-dried ash are used measuring 1½ × ½ inches and 1½ × ⅝ inch, respectively. As the bends are relatively slight, no problems would be expected from this operation. An allowance is made in the length to leave spare material for trimming back to the required size. This serves as a precaution against splitting and spring-back after the workpieces are released from the mold.

After the workpieces are removed from the steam box, they are placed between the two halves of the mold prepared with sash clamps arranged ready to apply pressure (6–3 and 6–4).

Gradually, the two halves of the mold are squeezed with the sash clamps, bringing the workpieces together to conform to the mold shape (6–5 to 6–7). A batten is nailed across the two halves of the mold at each end, to retain

*It is worth pointing out that the terms "mold," "form," and "former" are interchangeable.

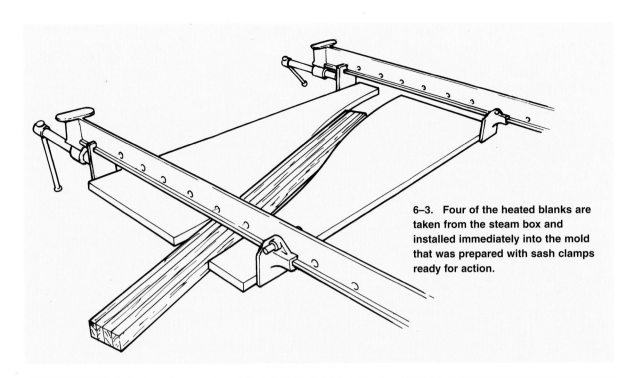

6–3. Four of the heated blanks are taken from the steam box and installed immediately into the mold that was prepared with sash clamps ready for action.

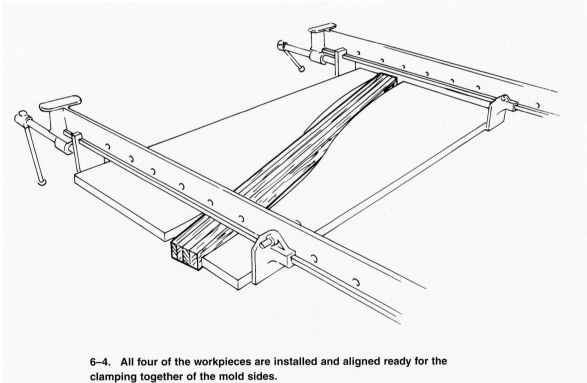

6–4. All four of the workpieces are installed and aligned ready for the clamping together of the mold sides.

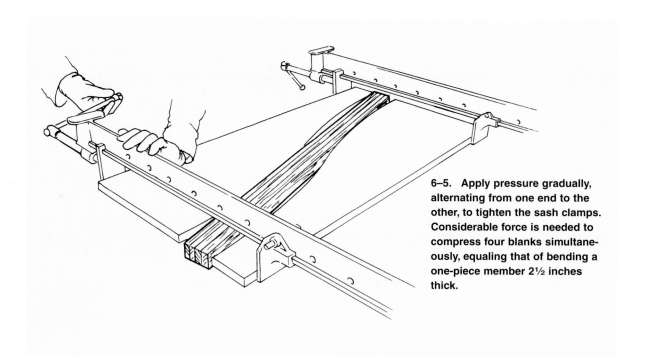

6–5. Apply pressure gradually, alternating from one end to the other, to tighten the sash clamps. Considerable force is needed to compress four blanks simultaneously, equaling that of bending a one-piece member 2½ inches thick.

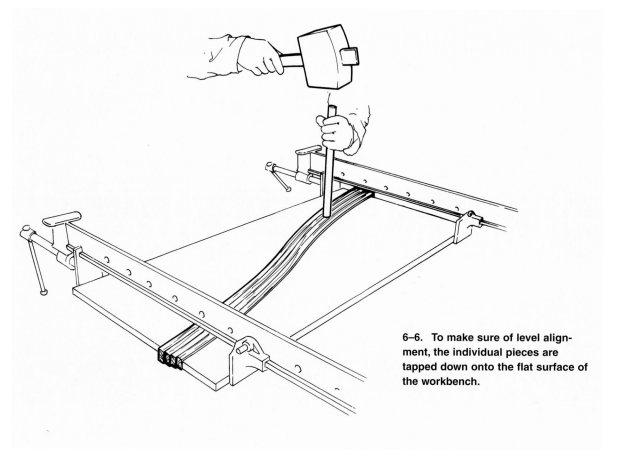

6–6. To make sure of level alignment, the individual pieces are tapped down onto the flat surface of the workbench.

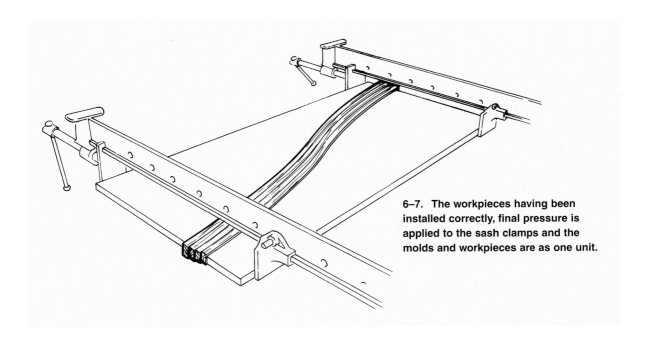

6–7. The workpieces having been installed correctly, final pressure is applied to the sash clamps and the molds and workpieces are as one unit.

the pressure after the sash clamps are removed (6–8), and the whole assembly is set aside for a few days until the wood is dry (6–9). This S-bend member was used in combination with the semicircular bends detailed in chapter 7 (6–10). That chapter contains drawings that show how two simple bends may be associated to produce a range of products (6–11).

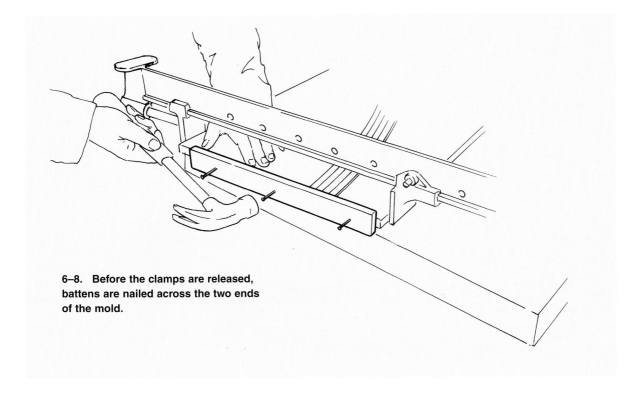

6–8. Before the clamps are released, battens are nailed across the two ends of the mold.

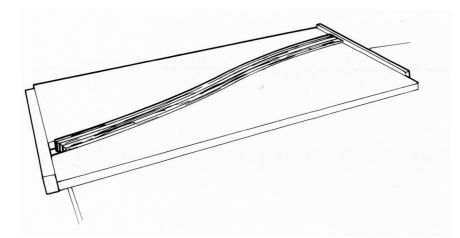

6–9. These battens will stay in place until the bends are dry.

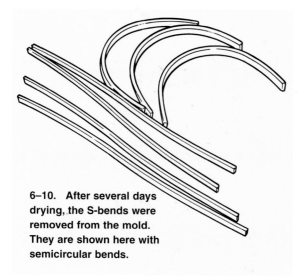

6–10. After several days drying, the S-bends were removed from the mold. They are shown here with semicircular bends.

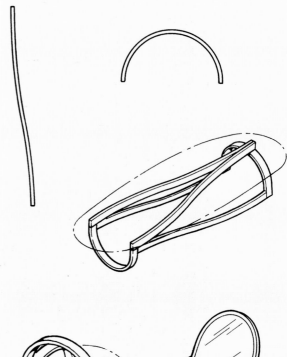

6-11. Simple bends can be used to produce a variety of items.

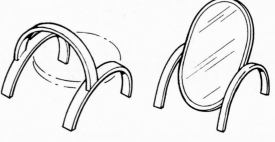

Chapter 7

BENDING EQUIPMENT

This chapter is devoted to describing a comprehensive range of specifically developed bending equipment based on traditional tools, but refined to suit the contemporary amateur craftsman. For the reader requiring additional information, write to Sterling Publishing Company, 387 Park Avenue South, New York, New York 10016.

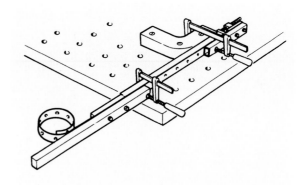

7–1. Clamped to the mold is the adjustable end of the workpiece/strap assembly; a clamp is applied to the free end to fix the strap to the workpiece.

STRAP CLAMPS

There is a workpiece/strap assembly available that consists of 1¼- and 2-inch-wide metal straps to which can be fitted an adjustable end stop (7–1). Adjustment of the end stop facilitates accurate fitting of the bending blank to ensure that there can be no stretching of the outer fibers during the bending operation (refer to "The Effect of Bending on Wood" on pages 41 and 42.)

S-BEND UNIT

With a capacity of up to 2 inches wide, this unit is fastened to a work board and clamps a section of the workpiece, allowing bends to be produced on either side of it, to make S-bend shapes (7–2 and 7–3).

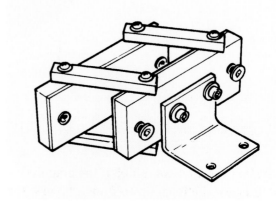

7–2. The S-bend unit that acts as a fixed clamp for bends incorporating change of direction.

CHANGE-OF-PLANE UNIT

In cases where a change of plane is needed, as found typically in bent-wood furniture designs, a change-of-plane unit is ideal (7–4). It follows that since the strap cannot be twisted, the strap must be cut in half or a second one applied.

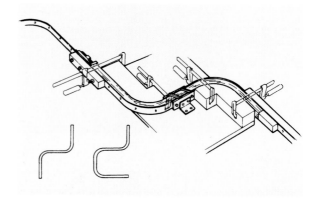

7–3. A typical arrangement using two molds, the strap clamp, and the S-bend unit. Inset are two examples of possible bent shapes with these components.

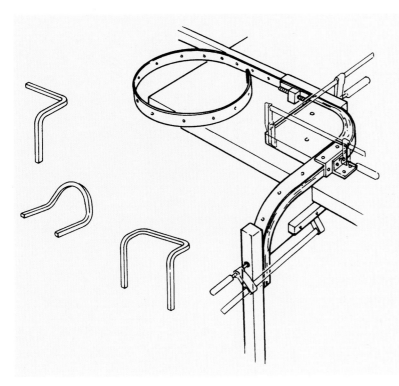

7–4. More complex bending is
accessible with the inclusion
of the change-of-plane unit,
which does exactly what its
name suggests. As the inset
shows, variations on the
theme are almost limitless.

BLOCK AND TACKLE

A system for applying efficient leverage when using heavy sections, up to 2-inch blanks, this block and tackle has customized fittings com-plimentary to the strap clamp assembly (7–5). If any hefty bending is needed, it is invaluable, especially with one-man operations.

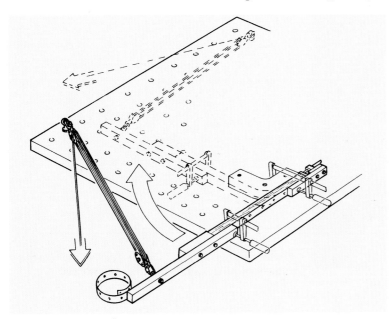

7–5. Repositioning of the anchor
point of the block is available by the
holes drilled into the workpiece. This
is to achieve a right angular pull
against the workpiece during the
bend.

ADVANTAGES OF A COMPLETE BENDING SYSTEM

There are complete, adaptable wood-bending kits available that provide many answers to the problems that face the amateur with a small workshop. It may be useful to demonstrate how one such strap-and-stop system is superior to free-bending methods, using the principles of "stretch prevention" as detailed in "The Effect of Bending on Wood" on pages 41 and 42. To do this, the following tests were performed. A mold was made to make up a 1¼-inch-thick × ⅝-inch-wide ash workpiece (7–6 and 7–7). It was screwed to a work board. The ash workpiece was sufficient in length to make a complete semicircle plus a little extra for trimming. To prevent any chance of the mold moving during the bending operation, it was clamped securely to the workbench.

Several blanks were loaded into the hot steam box, steamed with a kettle. After 20 minutes, one of the blanks was removed from the steam box and brought to the mold. Bending commenced, but the workpiece broke

7–7. The mold was cut to just over a semi-circle and a recess sawn to accommodate a clamp. It was screwed to a work board.

7–6. A mold was made from two layers of plywood, to make up a plank about 1¼ inches thick, and inscribed with a semicircle of about 9 inches radius.

(7–8 to 7–10). This emphasizes the point that wood may be considered for all practical purposes as nonstretchable. If anything more than slight bends are needed, the wood may break, without a strap to compress the fibers on the outer surface of the bend.

Next, a second test was made using a strap clamp/assembly (7–11). The stops and strap were assembled and adjusted to suit the workpiece length before the steam box was loaded. The results were a successful bending operation and an intact workpiece (7–12 to 7–16).

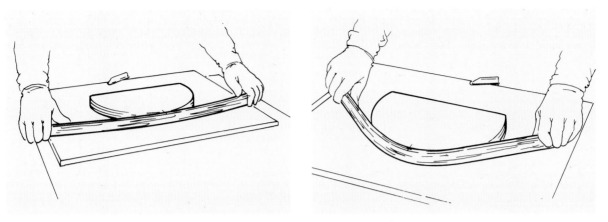

7–8 and 7–9.   After the blank centerline was aligned with the marked center on the mold, the bend was commenced by pulling each end, held in gloved hands.

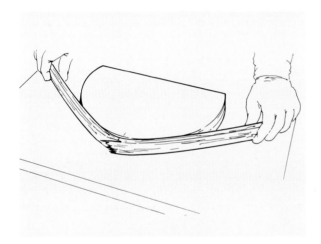

7–10.   All went well until approximately 90 degrees was approached, that is 45 degrees on each side of the center. At this point the workpiece broke, rupturing on the centerline with the fibers bursting from the outer surface.

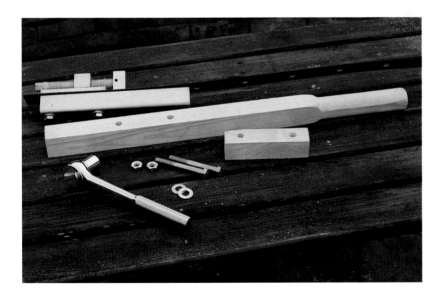

7–11.   Components of the strap clamp with user-made grip and fixed stop made of plywood.

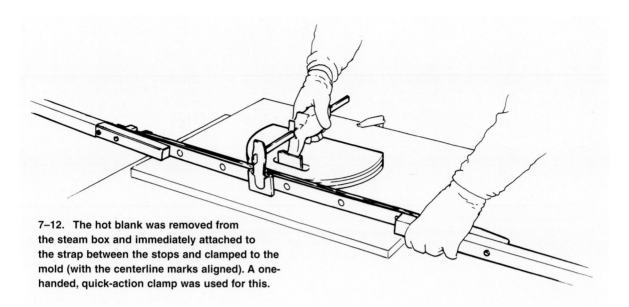

7–12. The hot blank was removed from
the steam box and immediately attached to
the strap between the stops and clamped to the
mold (with the centerline marks aligned). A one-
handed, quick-action clamp was used for this.

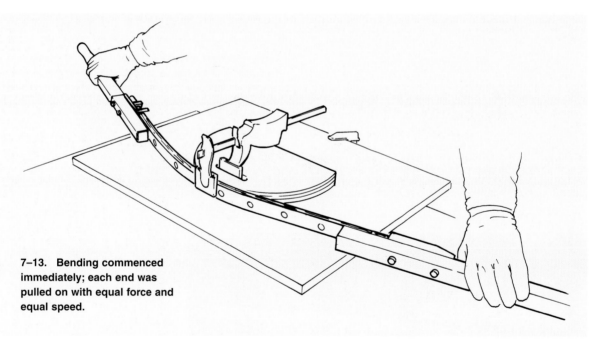

7–13. Bending commenced
immediately; each end was
pulled on with equal force and
equal speed.

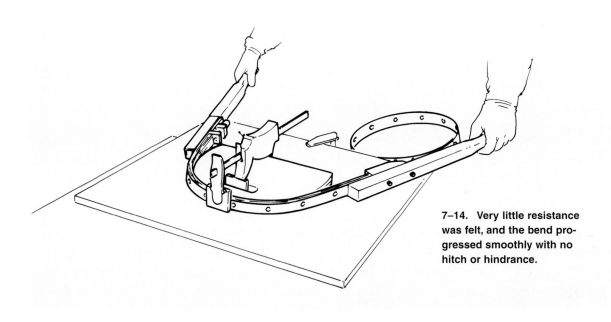

7–14. Very little resistance was felt, and the bend progressed smoothly with no hitch or hindrance.

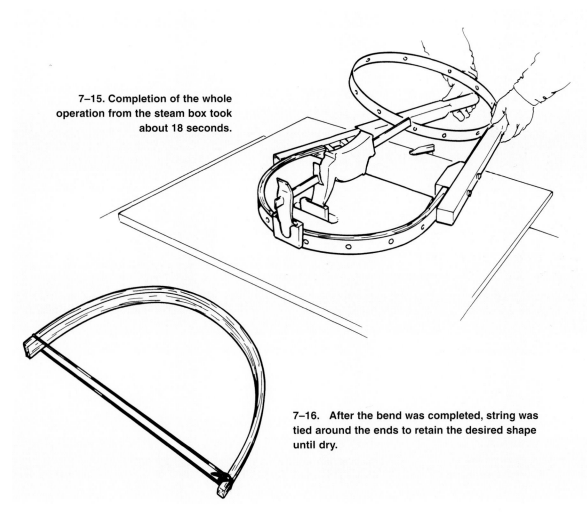

7–15. Completion of the whole operation from the steam box took about 18 seconds.

7–16. After the bend was completed, string was tied around the ends to retain the desired shape until dry.

PART TWO

Wood-Bending Projects and Demonstrations

Chapter 8

BENDING SIDES
FOR OVAL BOXES

Oval boxes are much-loved utensils preserved in the fabric of American rustic crafts (8–1). They are made in a vast range of sizes. The largest are big enough to contain several hats, and some are so small they are the size of pocket pillboxes.

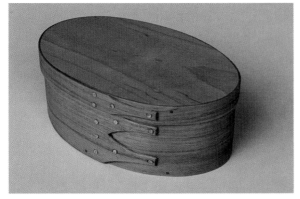

8–1. A fine example of an oval box after the Shaker style. The sides are made from maple, and the top and base from cherry.

A wide variety of hardwoods are suitable for this type of box, no doubt depending in the past on what was growing near the workshop. While there is some room for individual ex-

pression in proportions or jointing, the oval box in its traditional design was believed by most to have been perfected by Shaker craftsmen.

Derek Hooper, an Englishman skilled in handcrafted wooden furniture and musical instruments, is shown in the following demonstration. His techniques are based on the methods and materials of John Wilson, a craftsman specializing in Shaker traditions. John Wilson's workshop in Charlotte, Michigan, supplies those hard-to-find bits and pieces essential to this type of work.

Medium-density fiberboard was used for the forms shown in the accompanying photographs, but any spare wood will do. Multiple layers are built up to the thickness required by the box design. If no band saw is available, the single layers can be cut separately and then laminated before final smoothing with conventional tools. A batten is screwed to the bottom of the form to enable it to be gripped in a bench vise for security when the sides and top bands are being bent against the form (8–2).

The material for the sides and top bands may be chosen from cherry, ash, pear, apple,

8–2. In the foreground are five forms, or cores, on which the box sides are shaped. The battens attached to the top of the forms will be used to hold them (inverted) in a bench vise for security during the bending operation.

maple, sycamore, or almost any other close-grained hardwood. Some superb effects may be achieved if decorative woods such as bird's-eye maple or lacewood are used. Softwoods may be used for the tops and bottoms of the boxes, with the proviso that color and texture should be considered when marrying the component parts for the sake of creating a harmonious appearance.

After the material is selected, the sides and top bands are smoothed and cut to width, length, and thickness. As to the latter dimension, some trials are advised using spare material of the kind chosen for the project. The sides must bend obligingly to the form and ac-

cept the copper tacks to hold the shape of the box; both operations should be achieved without splitting the wood. A sawn veneer of standard thickness may work without further attention, apart from cutting it to length and width. Obviously, it is better to finish the materials to a respectable smoothness before bending to reduce the problem after the box is made.

A template is prepared to the required shape of the "fingers," the decorative ends of the sides and top bands (8–3). The outline of the template is traced on the end of the strips and the fingers are cut out with a sharp-bladed knife (8–4). An alternative method of

8–3. A "finger" template made from transparent plastic sheet, perforated to indicate the positions intended for the insertion of the tacks.

8–4. Cutting out the fingers on the end of the box using a sharp-bladed knife. A resilient surface such as a vinyl floor tile is used as a base on which to cut out the shapes.

cutting the fingers is shown in 8–5. If the wood is of an unwilling disposition, wetting it with warm water may help to shape the fingers satisfactorily.

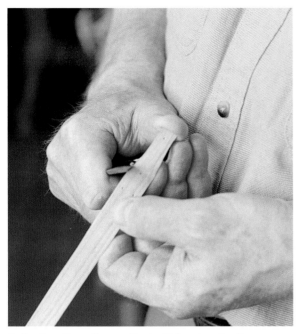

8–5. An alternative method of trimming the fingers, using a handheld carving technique. The single finger at the end of the top band is being trimmed.

As with other bending operations the wood needs to be heated, and the easiest method for heating sides and top bands is with hot water. Steam will work but bearing in mind the relatively small sizes and thin material, water has the advantage. Any container of sufficient size will do for this job, provided that it will withstand boiling water. It is best to use an oversize trough because more water than necessary will be needed to immerse the strips (8–6).

After covering the strips with boiling water, they are left soaking for about 20 minutes. Timing is not critical and, if after the first trial the material seems stubborn, a further soak in freshly boiled water may help. Normally the procedure is straightforward with little difficulty.

8–6. An ideal plastic trough, intended for use as a window box for plants, is being used to soak the sides and top bands. It is big enough to hold many pieces, but not so big as to waste hot water.

The side is removed from the hot water (after 20 minutes, it is not too hot to handle with bare hands) and is brought to the form. In the bending operation, the benefits of the vise-held form will become obvious since both hands are used to wrap the side around the form (8–7). The plain end is placed first on the form and held there firmly; then the other end with the fingers is brought around the form. A close fit is maintained as the softened material

8–7. Wrapping the hot, wet side around the form.

is wrapped around until the finger end is brought into place, overlapping itself to complete the box side.

When the side is wrapped completely and the shape is formed without gaps in the periphery, a pencil mark is made where the two layers cross (8–8). This is for reference later for accurate realignment when the sides are removed from the form (8–9).

It is now necessary to secure the ends of the side and fix it in the required oval shape. Copper tacks are used for this job, specific sizes for specific thickness of material (8–10).

Tack length is important, because after the tack is inserted through both layers, the point is deformed by a riveting action to produce a "head" that prevents withdrawal. This holds the two layers securely and permanently without the need for glue.

An anvil is needed to complete the riveting operation. It may be improvised from a piece of metal pipe; steel or iron will also do (8–11). The pipe is simply held between two wooden jaws and clamped to the bench top. Clean up the surface of the pipe with an abrasive to avoid staining of the material when it is brought to the anvil.

8–8. A pencil mark is made to allow realignment of the shaped side after it is removed from the form.

8–9. Aligning the pencil marks on the inner and outer layers of the bent sides.

8–10. Tiny tacks are set aside in readiness for the riveting operation.

8–11. An improvised anvil made from a piece of steel pipe held between two pieces of wood. The wood was first drilled to the diameter of the pipe, split into two, and reassembled with screws to grip the pipe.

Set up the anvil, a light hammer, and tacks so they are ready to fix the ends of the strips as soon as they are bent and marked. At this stage, it is wise to examine the bent material to detect any signs of cracking across the grain, or splitting along the grain, that might have occurred due to the stresses caused by bending.

Riveting is an uncomplicated affair provided that the marks are aligned accurately and the tack locations are clearly visible (8–12). Some care needs to be taken when hammering the tacks, which, being made of relatively soft copper, may bend sideways and become de-

formed. If this happens, it is best to discard the tack rather than try to recover its shape and replace it with a good one.

While the ends of the side are kept together and laid on the anvil, they are held with one hand while the sharp tack is pressed into the wood at a marked position. The tack is as sharp as a pin and enters the wood easily. As the hammer strikes the tack through both the layers, the tack point is driven against the anvil and deforms into an irremovable head. The workpiece shown in 8–13 is a top band.

8–12. This is the riveting operation showing the anvil clamped to the bench top.

8–13. Here there are eight rivets holding the fingers and ends securely.

While the freshly bent side is still "green" and flexible, it is necessary to allow it to dry without becoming misshaped. This calls for the use of a "shaper," made to the identical shape of the form and therefore a perfect fit in the riveted side. It is inserted, temporarily, into both the top and bottom of the newly bent sides, and the assembly is left to dry (8–14).

The workpiece must be thoroughly dried, the time required varying, depending on the local ambient temperature, humidity, airflow, etc., but at least a day is recommended. After the drying period, the shapers are removed and the bottom of the box may be fitted. Using the same shape established by the original form, the bottom is cut, finished smoothly, and inserted into the oval sides (8–15).

Wooden retaining pegs will be driven into the sides and bottom through pilot holes. To accomplish the drilling of the pilot holes, a simple jig is used, combining a mini-power tool fitted with a drill bit to match the diameter of the pegs and a simple wooden clamp (8–16). This holds the power tool in the horizontal position while the workpiece is guided manually to perform the drilling operation. A system of stack-

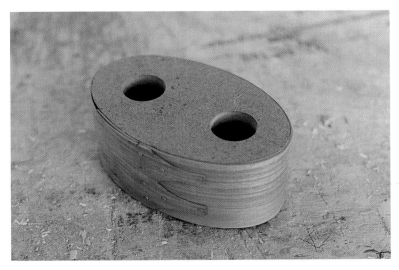

8–14. Shapers have been inserted into the top and bottom of the sides to keep the shape as the wood dries out from the soaking. The two holes in the shaper are for ease of handling it into and out of the assembly.

8–15. A carefully prepared bottom should enter the sides without undue difficulty.

ing layers underneath the box is used to raise it correctly to the level needed to drill the holes, and it is then slid on the horizontal platform.

Good-quality wooden toothpicks make suitable retaining pegs, and these may be cut in half to make two pegs from each pick. These make ideal wooden "nails" that are pointed at one end and flat at the other (8–17). A trial is advised to ensure that the drill chosen for the pilot holes produces the correct fit. It should neither be too small to risk splitting the sides nor too loose so as to fall out.

Any excess length of peg left protruding from the box side should be cut off and trimmed back to the surface (8–18). Any abrasive should suffice for this job, but not so coarse as to spoil the finish on the smooth sides.

A similar procedure is used to make the top, using the bottom of the box to establish its size and shape (8–19).

8–16. A clamp made from spare material holds the mini-power tool. It was produced by drilling a hole of suitable diameter between two pieces clamped together and then reconnecting the pieces with two screws and wing nuts. This assembly was then screwed to the platform to make the drilling jig. It is advisable to clamp the platform to the bench top when operating the drill for safety and security.

8–17. Hammering home the wooden pegs.

8–18. Smoothing the excess pegs protruding from the surface of the side.

8–19. Derek Hooper with one of his oval boxes.

Chapter 9

WALKING STICKS

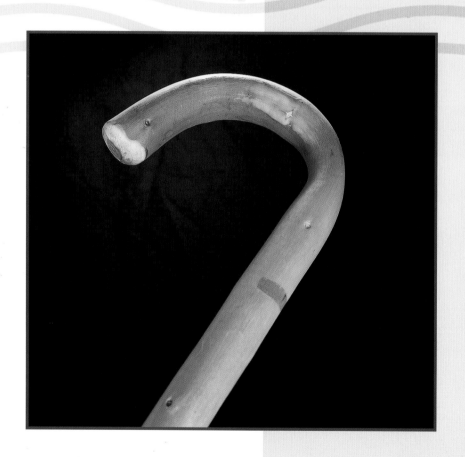

Making walking sticks with curved handles is a tradition whose origins go back to the time when it flourished as a rustic craft in nineteenth-century England (9–1). From this, it grew into a significant industry supplying sticks for the wounded of two world wars. Not merely as an aid to walking, sticks may be fashioned to special shapes to suit other purposes, such as to help in mountain climbing or as crooks used for the control of sheep.

Few factories have survived the recent change to metal sticks; one that has is the Phoenix Walking Stick Company of Nailsworth in Gloucestershire, England. Although some of their techniques have been mechanized for the sake of efficiency, the process involves mainly the application of hand skills, similar in principle to its traditional origins. The information in this section describes and illustrates the stick-making production cycle at the Phoenix factory. The information in the following section describes and illustrates how to bend sticks in the home workshop.

Sweet chestnut sticks are supplied young and "green," mostly from local coppices, but a small percentage is imported from Spain (9–2).

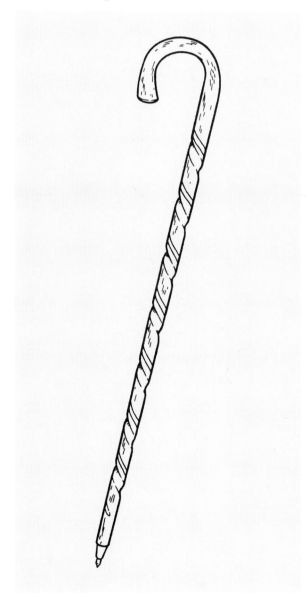

9–1. Walking stick.

9–2. Sticks brought into the workshop in readiness for bending. Some have yet to be debarked. This will be done by boiling and stripping.

The sticks are boiled on arrival to facilitate the removal of the bark. When they enter the production line they are steamed for about 20 minutes in readiness for bending. Several steam chests are used to heat up dozens of sticks sequentially in readiness for a continuous bending operation (9–3). A machine is used to bend the handle (9–4 and 9–5) and, while it is still hot, the shaft is straightened if necessary (9–6). This latter operation is judged by eye and performed by applying leverage discreetly in a simple slotted beam.

After dipping in bleach, the sticks are transferred to an oven for drying (9–7), following which they are inspected carefully for flaws, trimmed to remove knots, and cut to length

9–3. Three steam chambers are working constantly in sequence, providing a supply of heated sticks ready for bending.

9–4. Bending of the stick handle is achieved by a hydraulically powered bending machine loaded and operated manually. Here the machine is seen partly through a bend.

9–5. The bending of the handle has been completed and it is tied with a cord to hold the shape until dry.

9–6. John Faulkner, the proprietor of the Phoenix Walking Stick Company, is seen straightening crooked sticks after the handles are bent and the sticks are still hot and pliant.

9–7. After the handles are bent and any undesirable bends have been corrected, a batch of sticks is loaded into an oven to hasten the drying time.

(9–8 to 9–12). A rubber ferrule is fitted to the straight end to prevent wear and to add security (9–13). To emphasize the efficiency of this enterprising company requires only to state that about half a dozen men produce around 4,000 walking sticks per week!

9–8. Racked up after returning from the oven, the dried sticks are ready for the trimming stages.

9–9. Overall length is trimmed on a small circular saw. Most sticks are made to a standard length regulated by the National Health Service, somewhat longer than average requirements, although many are shortened later to suit individual needs.

9–10. As might be expected from the information given elsewhere in earlier chapters, the handle is bent overlong and its length is trimmed at the same station as the length of the stick itself.

9–11. Minor nodules protruding above the surface of the stick are removed to leave it smooth to the touch.

9–12. A rotary cutter is used to shape the end of the handle, leaving it clean and rounded.

9–13. Fitted with its stout rubber foot for added security, the Phoenix walking stick is ready for service.

BENDING STICKS IN THE HOME WORKSHOP

For the home craftsman without factory facilities, the following is a similar process, based on the old craft.

First, determine which of the heating methods is most appropriate from the earlier chapters, and then continue as follows.

Selection of Materials

Fortunately, a wide range of woods is suitable, including chestnut, ash, hazel, holly, and cherry. It is generally preferred to remove the bark from walking sticks, and this is best done when the stock is fresh to avoid the need to boil. Any sticks with prominent knots or even the slightest cracks should be rejected. Small knots and nodules can be trimmed off, but this is best left until the stick is finished and dry.

Give or take a bit, lengths and diameters of walking sticks will be very similar, regardless of the kind of wood chosen. If the handle is bent at the wider end, the natural taper in the stick helps the balance. Up to 1¼ inch in diameter at its widest would work for a heavy stick, with an average of about 1 inch being most usual. Much less than this and the stick might be regarded as too weak to be reliable.

Preparation of Material

If the finished length of stick is established, from the bottom to the top of the handle, another 12 inches should be added to make the bend, assuming this is to be an inside radius of about 1½ inches (9–14). After cutting the blank to the prepared length, a small notch should be cut near the end to be bent, to secure the retaining cord.

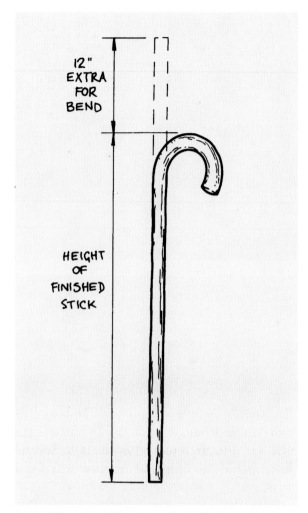

9–14. When the finished length of stick is decided upon, a 12-inch allowance is added for the bend and trimming. It is best to err on the side of generosity; after all, it is easy to cut off any unwanted portion.

Bending Equipment

A very simple arrangement is sufficient for bending the handles of walking sticks, easily made by the user and just as well, because such equipment is unlikely to be available from a tool supplier!

A peg-and-disc handle-bending jig is efficient and detailed in 9–15. A conventional woodworking vise attached to a workbench is adequate for holding the peg-and-disc jig. The

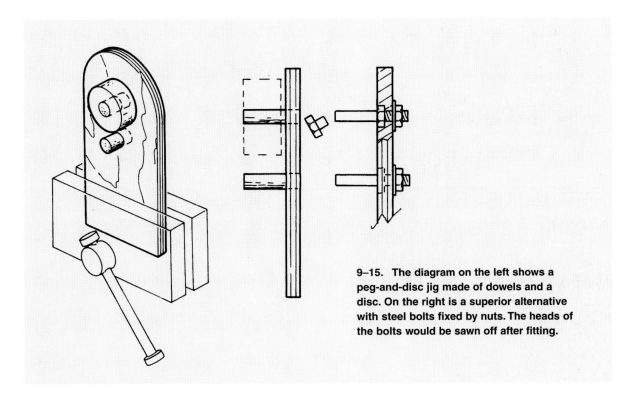

9–15. The diagram on the left shows a peg-and-disc jig made of dowels and a disc. On the right is a superior alternative with steel bolts fixed by nuts. The heads of the bolts would be sawn off after fitting.

disc should be free running on the upper 1-inch dowel so that after bending the handle the stick and disc are removed as one unit. Several discs should be prepared in readiness for a batch production. As an alternative to the wooden dowels, a metal dowel may be used made as shown with bolts as shown in the illustration.

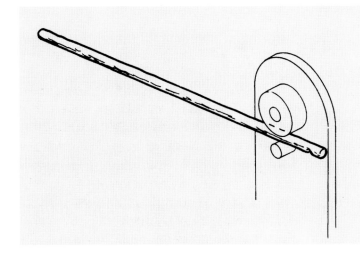

9–16. Locked in the bench vise, the jig is ready for use.

Bending Operation

After the workpiece is removed from the heat process, the end of the stick to be bent is placed in the jig between the peg and the disc (9–16). (Note: it is normal to use the thicker end of the stick for the handle.) Pressure is brought against the disc by the stick as it is effectively "wrapped" around it, following its circular profile (9–17).

The stick is taken to a few degrees past 360, to allow for spring-back, and a loop of string is tied around it as a retainer to temporarily hold in this position (9–18). The bent stick can then be removed from the jig still attached to the disc, upon which it is allowed to remain until it is dry.

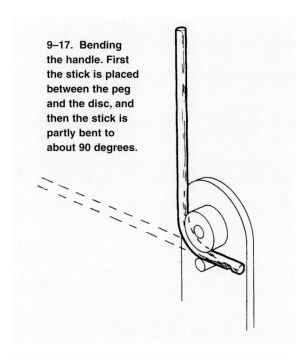

9–17. Bending the handle. First the stick is placed between the peg and the disc, and then the stick is partly bent to about 90 degrees.

9–19. A kettle may be used to pour boiling water over the stick. If contained in a bucket, the stick can be held for a time in the hot water to prolong the contact.

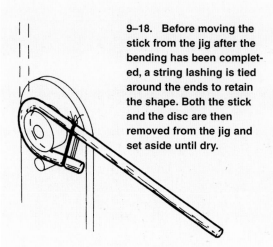

9–18. Before moving the stick from the jig after the bending has been completed, a string lashing is tied around the ends to retain the shape. Both the stick and the disc are then removed from the jig and set aside until dry.

If hot sand or boiling water was used for the handle-heating process, it is possible to soften the straight part of the stick for the correction of slight errors of curves in its length. A kettle of hot water may be poured over the stick with the end standing in a bowl to collect the water as it runs down (9–19). This should be sufficient to soften the wood for slight corrective straightening.

Finishing the Walking Stick

Assuming the workpiece is considered straight and the string clamp is secure, the stick may be set aside until it is dry. Note: just because the stick is cold, which it will quite quickly become, does not mean it is dry. Views differ on the subject, but it is easy enough to verify when the stick has reached a balanced moisture content by weighing it daily and recording the weight loss. It may be assumed that when little change in the weight is discernible, the stick is dry, nominally speaking, and should therefore retain its shape, within a few degrees, when the string clamp is released. If the weighing procedure seems like too much trouble, simply wait a week or two before removing the string.

Now cut both ends to length, trim off any protrusions, and add the rubber ferrule. Any hard-wearing varnish may be applied for decoration or as a preservative, though many stick-makers prefer the natural look of the wood to acquire a patina gradually with the passage of time.

Chapter 10

BOAT RIBS

This chapter details the whole technique of steaming, bending, and fitting mahogany boat ribs into a traditional dinghy. Two student boat builders under the direction of their tutor at Lyme Regis International School of Boatbuilding were the demonstrators. In charge of the project was tutor Bob Forsyth, master boat builder, ship surveyor, and author.

An adjustable-length, double-type, "one-inside-the-other" steam box—as described in Chapter 4—was set up in readiness to receive the ribs, these being prepared to size, about ¾ × ⅜ inch with the outside corners chamfered (10–1). The chamfering was to make less work for cleaning up the surface of the ribs after fitting them to the inside of the hull. To facilitate ease of handling and manipulation during the fitting, the ribs were left overlong.

Steam was generated by a high-power, industrial wallpaper stripper connected to the steam box (10–2). After about a half hour, the box was full of steam and its outside surface hot

10–1. A fine example of a double-box steam chest, with the inner box slide inside the outer to suit the length of the workpieces; in this case, they were both boat ribs. Chapter 4 describes how to use this type of steam box.

10–2. An industrial steam generator was used to provide the steam.

to the touch. The ribs were loaded into the steam box (10–3) and left for about 20 minutes, during which time a few clamps and a couple of hammers were gathered on site.

The dinghy was almost completed except for the few remaining ribs to be fitted in this session. In accordance with the policy of highest-quality workmanship, some ribs had been removed to improve either the quality of the rib or the fitting. Trestles had been arranged on which to rest the hull to raise its gunwales to about waist height for convenience of working.

At the appropriate moment, the end door was opened briefly to remove one rib and closed immediately after (10–4). Wood this narrow and thin cools quickly and the demonstrators had no difficulty in handling the rib straight from the steam box. However, it should be remembered that these were experienced, hardened hands and it is better for the beginner to err on the side of caution; in other words, wear gloves.

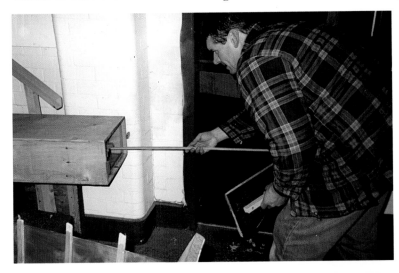

10–3. Ribs were loaded into the steam box; an attempt was made to keep them separate to ensure uniform exposure to the steam.

10–4. After about 20 minutes in the steam box, the first rib was removed and the door replaced in the end of the box to retain the steam.

The rib was brought to the hull and placed in position (10–5). A man on either side grasped the ends of the rib and pressed it into the hull, forcing it to take the shape of the planking, as if into a mold (10–6). C-clamps were used, with gentle force, to attach each end of the rib at the gunwales (10–7). Using a small hammer, the ends were then tapped to force the rib securely into the internal shape of the hull (10–8). Finally, the clamps were tightened to hold the rib securely. Total time for the operation from opening the steam box door to final tightening of the clamp was 20 seconds! Fitting the second and third ribs took less than 15 seconds each, illustrating the significance of practice (10–9).

Later, just for fun, Bob gave a demonstration of how, with ideal conditions, sound material, and correct steaming, it was possible to bend a piece of 1-inch-thick ash to a radius of about 12 inches with bare hands and his knee (10–10 and 10–11)! There was a look on his face that implied, "Don't try this at home, kids!"

10–5. The hot and flexible rib was pressed firmly and smoothly into place and one end was clamped lightly to the gunwale.

10–6. With one end secured, the rib was pressed into place against the planking.

10–7. As soon as the free end of the rib was pressed into place, it was also lightly clamped to the gunwale.

10–8. Because the clamps were not tightened fully, extra force was applied to the rib by tapping the end with a hammer. Both ends were treated similarly, resulting in an extremely tight-fitting rib.

10–9. A fine example of a fully planked and ribbed dinghy made by students of the Lyme Regis International School of Boatbuilding.

10–10 and 10–11. This 1-inch-thick piece of ash can be bent to a radius of 12 inches with bare hands and a knee. This should not be tried at home!

10–11.

Chapter 11

CHAIR BACKS

It is fairly safe to assume that a new wood-bending application was developed when "stools" were given backs and thus became "chairs." No serious historical analysis is intended at this point—other specialized publications deal with that subject—but a glance at furniture design and its development through traditional crafts would suggest this to be true.

At its best, the bent chair back is at once economical of material and labor, strong and efficient, functional and elegant. There are boundless variations of style, but probably the most widely recognized is the English Windsor chair. Of the many contemporary exponents of the craft of chair-making and of the Windsor in particular is lecturer, author, and craftsman Jack Hill.

Here follows a demonstration of a typical bending session, part of a chair-making course given by Jack, with a group of students at West Dean College in West Sussex, England (11–1).

Local grown ash, prepared to about a 1½-inch-square section, was the material chosen to produce traditional Windsor chair backs using steam and a strap-and-stop bending technique, as described in chapter 3. The wood blanks were air-dried to about 25 percent moisture content and enclosed in a polyethylene envelope before being brought into the workshop (11–2). The precaution of careful storage in its own plastic environment was to prevent the wood from rapidly drying with all the attendant problems of developing warp, shakes, etc. (refer to "Bending Characteristics of Wood" on pages 15 to 21).

Only when the bending session began was the plastic cover removed and the blank workpieces chosen from the bundle. Although the samples had already been set aside for the purpose of chair-back production, each piece was carefully examined for flaws before the final choice was made (11–3).

11–1. A fine display selected from the collection of traditional chairs made by Jack Hill. The backs of these chairs were created using wood-bending techniques.

11–2. Chair-back blanks enveloped in polyethylene to prevent drying too quickly.

11–3. Choosing blanks suitable for the chair-back bending project.

Previously, preparation of the worksite had included laying out, on a sturdy workbench, the jig and mold around which the blank would be bent (11–4), some clamps, and the strap-

11–4. Clamp-and-mold system for the production of slats for ladder-back chairs.

and-stop equipment (11–5). The metal strap was of stainless steel fitted with hardwood stops (refer to "The Effect of Bending on Wood" on pages 41 and 42).

Measurements were made to establish the exact length to which the blanks would be cut to fit snugly between the end stops fitted to the straps. Following this, the blanks were tied onto the strap for ease of handling to and from the steam box (11–6).

Nearby an electrically heated urn was three-quarters filled with water and switched on to boil (11–7). Over this was placed a board with a square hole to match that in the bottom of the steam box. The steam box was then placed on the top of the covered urn with the holes aligned to admit the steam, and a blanket was draped over the box for insulation (11–8). Cloth wads were used to block the ends of the steam box.

Two straps fitted with blanks were loaded into the steam box when it was hot and filled with steam (11–9). It is a sound principle to heat up the strap as well as the blank, since loss of time and precious heat are both saved when transferring these items from the box to the bending jig.

A practice run was made with the equipment in which speed—always a great contributor to the success of the bending operation—and effi-

11–5. Jack arranges the bending kit, strap, mold, and clamps to prepare for a smooth operation.

11–6. Two blanks were fitted and tied to the stainless-steel straps. Careful measurements ensured that the blanks just fitted inside the stops to ensure close contact between the strap and the workpiece.

11–7. An urn, with a spare standing by, was already heating up for steam generation.

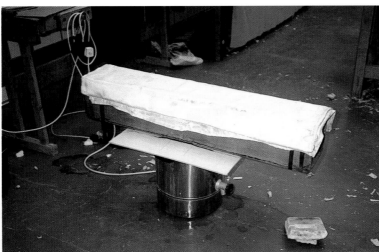

11–8. A plywood steam box was placed on the urn. In the bottom of the box was a hole to admit the steam.

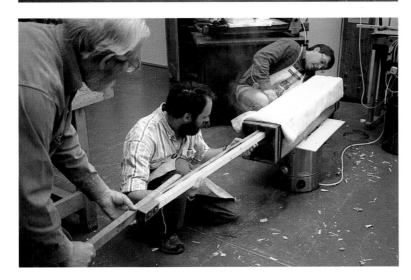

11–9. Both of the prepared straps with their blanks were loaded into the steam box.

ciency were emphasized (11–10). Everybody involved was instructed meticulously on his or her function, both individually and collectively.

Following the practice, one of the blanks was removed from the steam box after about 40 minutes duration and brought to the jig by two men, one at each end, with gloved hands.

As the blank/strap assembly was placed in position on the jig, a third person clamped it at its center to the mold (11–11). As soon as the C-clamp was secured, the bend was commenced, smoothly and without pause (11–12 and 11–13).

When the bend was completed and the blank was brought into contact with the entire mold, a fourth person applied a sash clamp across the ends to hold it in the position temporarily (11–14). A cord was lashed around the two ends for long-term security and the sash

11–10. Steaming continued as the group practiced the bending sequence.

11–11. Clamping the strap-and-blank assembly to the mold.

11–12. Both ends were moved simultaneously to balance the compressive force on each side of the mold.

11–13. A smooth action was maintained without pause to gradually bring together the two ends of the workpiece.

11–14. After the completion of the bend, a sash clamp was placed across the two ends for security.

clamp was removed (11–15). There was sufficient slack in the bend to allow removal of the back, still attached to the strap, with which it would remain until dry (11–16).

To ensure retention of the shape after the removal of the strap, a batten would be fixed across the open ends, by nails, until the back was needed for another fine Windsor chair (11–17 and 11–18).

11–15. A cord was lashed around the ends of the bent workpiece to enable its removal from the mold.

11 -16. A successful operation, a completed bend, and a happy Jack!

11–17. Various chair backs, differing in size and type, held in shape with battens as they dry out.

11–18. Rounded blanks that will be held in molds until dry.

11–18. Seen on a sidewalk in Harrow, England, here is a fine example of bentwood members made from laminated beech. No label or maker's name was attached.

Appendices

WOOD-BENDING CHARTS AND TABLES

This section contains pertinent information concerning specific items to be wood-bent and the preferred methods of heating and bending, suitable species of wood to use, and minimum radius achievable.

Table 1

Bent Items and Suitable Methods of Heating*

Items	Hot water	Hot steam	Hot air	Hot pipe
Walking sticks (chapter 9**)	x	x		
Slats for trugs or gardening baskets (chapter 4)	x	x	x	x
Boat planking (chapters 1 and 2)	x	x		
Boat ribs (chapters 4 and 10)	x	x		
Water skis (chapter 3)	x	x		
Chair backs (chapters 4 and 11)	x	x		
Sides for musical instruments (chapters 2, 3, 4, and 5)	x	x	x	x
Linings for musical instruments (chapters 3 and 5)			x	x
Sides for Shaker-type boxes (chapter 8)	x	x	x	x
Sides for traditional boxes	x		x	

*Methods marked with an x can be used to heat wood for that particular item.
**This indicates chapter in which bending methods for that particular item are discussed.

Table 2

Bent Items and Appropriate Methods of Bending

Items	Strap & stop	Clamp & mold	Clamp & glue	Clamp & nail	Lamination	Kerfing
Walking sticks (chapter 9)		X				
Slats for trugs or gardening baskets (chapter 4)				X		
Boat planks (chapters 1 and 2)		X		X		
Boat ribs (chapters 4 and 10)		X		X		
Water skis (chapter 3)		X			X	
Chair backs (chapters 4 and 11)	X				X	
Sides for Shaker-type boxes (chapter 8)						
Sides for traditional boxes						

Table 3

Bent items and recommended wood species

Items	Beech	Oak	Ash	Chestnut	Cherry	Sycamore	Teak	Rosewood	Lime	Willow	Maple
Walking sticks			x	x							
Slats for gardening baskets	x		x	x	x	x				x	x
Boats planks		x	x				x				
Boat ribs		x	x	x							
Water skis	x		x	x		x					x
Chair backs	x	x	x	x	x	x					x
Sides for musical instruments					x	x		x			
Linings for musical instruments									x	x	x

Table 4

Radius achievable with selected wood, assuming it is 1 inch thick, heated by steam, and bent with a supporting strap.

Wood species Common name	Minimum radius in inches
Ash, American	4.5
Ash, European	2.5
Beech	2.0
Cherry, European	2.0
Chestnut, Sweet	3.0
Douglas Fir	15.0
Ebony	10.0
Elm	1.5
Greenheart	18.0
Hemlock	18.0
Hickory	2.0
Hornbeam	4.0
Larch	12.0
Lime	14.0
Mahogany, African	36.0
Mahogany, American	12.0
Oak, American White	1.0
Oak, European	2.0
Olive	12.0
Pine	36.0
Plane (European) Sycamore (American)	2.0
Spruce	36.0
Teak	18.0
Walnut, European	1.0
Western Red Cedar	35.0
Yew	8.5

GLOSSARY

There are several definitions applicable to many of the words that appear below, but only those meanings are given that are relevant to the subject of bending and their use within this book.

Air dried Timber that has been allowed to dry by circulation of air.

Bending iron A metal cylinder, hollow or solid, normally heated by electricity.

Blank Any workpiece that is prepared for a further stage of work.

Cambium The layer found beneath the bark of a tree.

Case hardened The surface of wood that has been dried out too quickly.

Cell A biological term referring to the smallest unit of an organism that may function independently.

Cellulose The main constituent of plant cell walls.

Clamp-and-mold Improvised equipment comprising clamps and a user-made mold.

Density Volumetric measure expressed in pounds per cubic foot.

Double-peg jig A simple box-like structure with two dowels inserted into holes in each side.

Dry weight Means the lowest weight achievable.

Fiber saturation point When the cell walls are saturated but there is no water within the cell cavity.

Form Another name for a mold, or former.

Galvanized A protective zinc coating on metal.

Grain Referring to the direction, size, and arrangement of fibrous elements in wood.

Green A term referring to freshly felled unseasoned wood.

Grown As in "grown" knee, a member formed by natural growth of a tree or limb.

Growth ring A layer of wood added in a season to the tree beneath the cambium.

Gunwale The upper edge of a ship's or boat's side.

Hot pipe Generic term for a heated cylinder used for heating thin wood sections.

Jig Any device made to guide, support, or control a workpiece or tool.

Kerf Width of cut made by a saw blade, not the blade width.

Kiln dried Timber that has been dried artificially in a heated chamber.

Laminate To bond together two or more layers with grain aligned in parallel.

Lignin Found as a bond between wood cells.

Luthier From the word "lute," taken to mean a maker of any stringed musical instruments.

Medium-density fiberboard (mdf) Man-made particleboard.

Moisture content This is expressed as a percentage of the dry weight of timber.

Moisture meter An instrument for measuring the amount of moisture contained in solids.

Mold A device used to give definitive shape to a malleable workpiece.

Neutral axis An imaginary line between extended and compressed axes.

Particleboard Sheet material made from wood chips.

Photosynthesis Light energy synthesizing carbon dioxide and water into organic compounds.

Plasticize To make soft or pliable.

Rib The side of a musical instrument or the inner support for boat planks.

Rive To split wood along its natural grain line, rather than sawing it.

Scarf A joint made by overlapping the ends of two lengths of timber with tapered joints.

Seasoned Dried timber of appropriate moisture content for its intended use.

Shake A defect in timber, appearing as a split, usually found at the end of a plank.

Slat A thin strip of wood, such as a rail in a chair back or the strips in a trug (gardening backet).

Specific gravity The ratio of the density of a substance to that of water.

Strap A metal strip used to support a workpiece in a bending operation.

Strap-and-stop Bending equipment comprising a metal strap with stops at each end.

Trug (gardening basket) A rustic basket made of wood slats with a natural stick handle.

Veneer Sawn or sliced wood generally less than $\frac{1}{16}$ inch thick.

METRIC EQUIVALENTS CHART

Inches to Millimeters and Centimeters

MM=Millimeters   **CM=Centimeters**

Inches	MM	CM	Inches	CM	Inches	CM
⅛	3	0.3	9	22.9	30	76.2
¼	6	0.6	10	25.4	31	78.7
⅜	10	1.0	11	27.9	32	81.3
½	13	1.3	12	30.5	33	83.8
⅝	16	1.6	13	33.0	34	86.4
¾	19	1.9	14	35.6	35	88.9
⅞	22	2.2	15	38.1	36	91.4
1	25	2.5	16	40.6	37	94.0
1¼	32	3.2	17	43.2	38	96.5
1½	38	3.8	18	45.7	39	99.1
1¾	44	4.4	19	48.3	48	101.6
2	51	5.1	20	50.8	41	104.1
2½	64	6.4	21	53.3	42	106.7
3	76	7.6	22	55.9	43	109.2
3½	89	8.9	23	58.4	44	111.8
4	102	10.2	24	61.0	45	114.3
4½	114	11.4	25	63.5	46	116.8
5	127	12.7	26	66.0	47	119.4
6	152	15.2	27	68.6	48	121.9

INDEX